T0124899

THE GIANTS OF SPORTSWEAR

# THE GIANTS OF SPORTSWEAR

## FASHION TRENDS THROUGHOUT THE CENTURIES

LANNOO

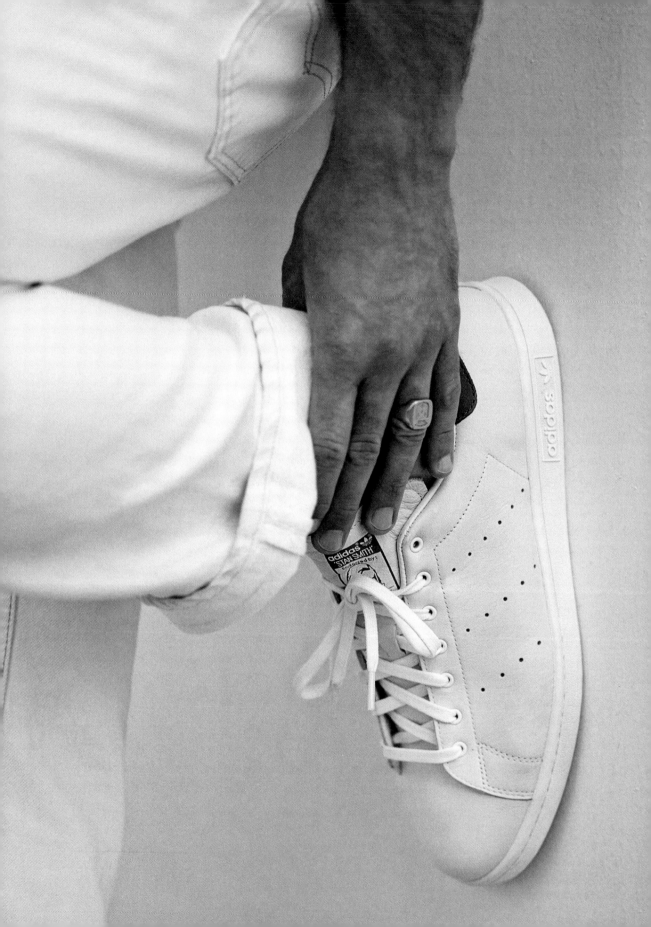

# INTRODUCTION

**What does sportswear tell us fashion-wise?** The Giants of Sportswear recounts the history of the big sportswear labels and highlights the work of designers who revolutionised the world of sportswear.

Looking at personalities in fashion past and present and the past makes us wonder why designers make us radiate and look elegant while doing sports. Sportswear has invaded the catwalks of Paris, Milan and New York, after ruling the streets of New York, Tokyo and London decades before. The world of fashion is open to female designers in sportswear. Stella McCartney, Beyonce, Rihanna make sportswear stylish and glamorous again. Today's sportswear makes us feel both comfortable and elegant, at one with ourselves and in shape. Sportswear has become our second skin. Fall under the spell of sportswear, read its history, feel its elegance and comfort, and get the vibe of sports!

Anyone can do sports. It's just a matter of picking the right sport and sporting outfit that suits you. But there's more to it than just the right pair of running shoes.

Especially for this book, I tested sports shoes from all the big sports labels and I can reveal the most successful pair of sport shoes: the Nike Air Force. The best designer sport shoes were Hogan Rebels. Adidas' Stan Smiths made the most successful comeback in sportswear. Most of my friends label Nike as the most popular brand. Nike's popularity may have something to do with the brand's concept of customising, which means that any client can choose his own model and colour of shoe… Every detail matters in the world of sportswear. Fashion is about recycling, sportswear is about inventing.

## Are your sneakers new or brand new?

Designers try to stun the press with the introduction of the most spectacular sportswear item. Sportswear turns fashion into a marriage between old and new. White is the new black in sportswear. The white elements in successive summer collections from Chloé, Lacoste and Moncler take us back to the early days of tennis, cricket and rugby. Pleated skirts in hockey and netball are favoured because they bring back the style of a British girls' school. There's now a declaration of love from high fashion to the world of sports and vice versa. Sportswear is the secret weapon of 'haute couture'. Why? Maybe because sportswear is about our first impression. Sportswear is linked to sports at a higher and more glamorous level. Sports and sportswear are one. Sport is versatile and rich. So is sportswear. We have definitely seen a glamorisation of sportswear during the last decade. Top Haute Couture brands Chanel, Vivienne Westwood, Dirk Bikkembergs, Prada and Rick Owens add elements from sportswear to their collections and 'turn the catwalk into an unlikely place of SPORT'*

Do we absolutely need to be fashionable when doing sports? Stella McCartney says YES in our interview in which she opens up about her collaboration with Adidas.
Sportswear is more than catwalk nonsense and is now finally being taken seriously. Women in the world of sports are becoming more important and open up a new field for players from the big sports labels. The regular sports lover may wonder about this new formality of sportswear and question why there is more to it than practical function and comfort.

A runner needs the correct clothes to perform at a peak level. Winning remains the ultimate goal. Winning in style is the goal of the sports star who becomes the face of the brand and when the brand is his face. That is also why brands have adopted a logo or created a name to make the brand live on in the minds of everyone. Within fashion it is time to think about the attraction of sportswear. Sportswear starts where fashion once started: from fabric to outfit. It is all about the material to create comfort. Sportswear is a billion dollar business and one of the most lucrative and important businesses in the world of fashion. Sportswear evokes our sense of comfort and style. That is why men and women buy sports items. They simply want or need them. That is the usual attitude towards sportswear. Now, however, unconventional approaches are in each new collection of sports outfits and sneakers

* Vogue editor Nick Remsen.

from the leading brands, or latest gadgets in the world of sports. The dividing line between sportswear, street wear and Haute Couture has disappeared. Sportswear has entered leading fashion magazines that seek and promise the perfect body and outfit. Let's get stylishly in shape and relax while reading the story of the giants of sportswear and be inspired by the leading ladies in the international sportswear arena. Listen to the message: 'A healthy mind in a healthy body,' and enjoy! Our body is our investment in the future. Hello sports, hello sportswear...

© Andy De Decker

# THE HISTORY OF SPORTSWEAR IN HIGH FASHION

**Is sportswear more than catwalk nonsense?**

Television and the internet bring sports into our world and convince us of the stylish aspect of sportswear today. Sports brands and Haute Couture labels have a clear vision of how to create and promote their clothes. The idea for this book started as I strolled through the streets of New York in 2010 and saw women going to the office in a suit with white sneakers. I saw how sneakers became more and more popular. Later on, I bumped into Zinedine Zidane on Sunset Boulevard in Los Angeles.

I walked into the Chanel shop and instead of finding Haute Couture dresses I found – to my surprise – a ski outfit in the middle of summer. Karl Lagerfeld said in 2014 that the only way to wear your Chanel couture gown was with a pair of trainers. 'The more fanciful the gown, the better,' he opined.

© Shutterstock

**When did sportswear and high fashion come together for the first time?**

Sportswear became a must-have item in the wardrobe of the 1920s elite who wanted to excel in horse racing, cycling, tennis and rugby, and embrace the comfort that sportswear promised. Coco Chanel was the first designer to adopt a sporty look and create *sportive* clothes for women of class. Her style and collections were influenced by sports such as horse racing, fishing and tennis. The famous Chanel suit was made of jersey taken from the sports industry. Her style was extremely masculine. Chanel introduced a more casual style for women and was an

© Chanel

early pioneer in sportswear. She was the first Parisian designer who knew that sport sells, well before American designers followed in her footsteps. She had discovered the secret weapon of the fashion industry in 'sportswear'. Chanel became a fashion prophet while saying, 'Simplicity is the key to all true elegance.' Chanel now has a popular perfume for men entitled, 'Allure Sport' and the Chanel brand focuses regularly on the sports theme with high-profile campaigns.

## What do sportswear and Haute Couture have in common?

Haute Couture refers to the profession of a traditional tailor who produces tailor-made clothes. This means clothes in the right size and shape for each customer. Tailor-made clothes and the attention to a high quality manufacturing process were synonymous. Charles Frederick Worth (1826-1895) was the first couturier in Paris to start a revolution in the world of fashion. Worth signed his clothes. His signature or label would then become a collector's item. This simple act hailed the start of branding. He also hired models instead of dolls to show his clothes. His work as a couturier is remembered today as his designs are still used in modern fashions. His name on clothes had the appeal for customers that the logo has on sports brands today.

The name Haute Couture is a protected trademark and refers to clothes which are made by hand. There are only eleven Parisian couturiers who are members of the Chambre Syndicale de la Haute Couture. To be a member of this elite group, every fashion house must employ at least twenty people and create at least 75 new designs. When we speak of Haute Couture we think of the hard work and beautiful creations of employees who embroider, sew, knit, design or print by hand. They work with all kinds of materials from leather to feathers. Top French couturier Maxime Simoens explained to me that the difference between Haute Couture and ready-to-wear is about distribution. Ready-to-wear is created for masses of women, whereas Haute Couture is created for just one woman in particular. This difference

Fashion happens. Sportswear happens a lot.

is also reflected in the higher price for Haute Couture, bespoke pieces. Simoens stresses that he always thinks of 'women in value' when creating his clothes.

In 1957, Dior described Haute Couture as 'the last treasure troves of pretty things. Haute Couture should not be accessible to everyone. It just should be there, so that we can feel its influence.'

Was this the end of Haute Couture? The final stages of the art date back to the swinging '60s when the American trend of the mass production of clothing became widespread. Fashion became open to everyone and not just to the 'happy few' who could afford a couturier who made the right clothes for the right occasion. Haute Couture and ready-to-wear were equally popular and had their own followers yet still influenced each other. Haute Couture reinvented itself by incorporating ready-to-wear, street wear and sportswear.

The success of sportswear goes back to the 1960s but had its breakthrough in the 1980s with the launch of Jane Fonda's legendary fitness video. Italian labels such as Kappa, Fila and Gucci paved the way for the success of sportswear today.

> When is something out of fashion? I think already before the first season.

Adidas, O'Neill, Champion, K-Way and Le Coq Sportif were internationally seen as pioneers in sportswear. Aerobics, sneakers, sunglasses, comfy leggings and T-shirts were part of the daily life of the power dressing '80s.

Sportswear trickled down to a larger, more mass audience and the media gave it the attention it deserved. Top models such as Cindy Crawford, Claudia Schiffer and Christy Turlington were the new *sportive* and curvy celebrities of their generation.

The bikini girl on the cover of *Sports Illustrated* became a superstar and had a promising career. The sporty image of the up-and-coming girl was part of the booming fashion scene. Everyone wanted to spend his/her money on sportswear and bought flashy clothes in the 1980s.

Sportswear became extremely important for the generations X & Y growing up in the '80s and '90s, belonging to hip hop and rap cultures and wearing hoodies and tracksuits.

Music and sports superstars the Beastie Boys, Run DMC and Michael Jordan turned the sports shoe into daily wear. Aerobics and jogging became the trend followed by a million amateur sportsmen. Sports became the aesthetics of a whole generation and sportswear became a true hype.

Thanks to the Internet and social media, sportswear has become an even bigger hype. Nowadays, bloggers and wannabe models have a record number of 'likes' on their Facebook, Instagram or Twitter pages, and people wonder what or who is next.

© Nike

Let's get back to where it all began…

In Britain, designer John Redfern was the tailor who made activewear for women on the sports field. His clothes were designed for tennis, yachting and archery but were worn by women all day.

In France, couturiers Patou and Chanel launched the trend of making sportswear sit next to high fashion and attracted attention from leading magazines such as *Harper's Bazaar* and *Vogue*.

*Vogue*, the world's leading fashion monthly publication, has long covered sport, and dedicated some of its front covers to female athletes and sporting heroins.

In 1929 *Vogue* also published the first ad for sportswear by Abercrombie and Fitch in which they showed the positive image of a girl in sportswear. The sports hype started for *Vogue* in The June Issue in 1940, merging the shape of the letters of the alphabet by artist Erté with sportswomen of the time.

The magazine has since then dedicated more and more pages to sports in both their summer and winter editions. *Vogue* often marvels in the world of sports and shows its readers how sports and fitness are part of people's health-conscious lives today. 'Sporty chic' makes us dream of ski resorts around the globe with multifunctional flashy items, and daring ski outfits in wintertime for skiing on and off piste.

Sportswear influences Haute Couture and Haute Couture influences sportswear. Belgium's first blogger and personal stylist Emma Gelaude comments: 'Stylish "comfy wear" has become a hot trend in which we love to invest a lot of money. Sport has become image, and image is supreme. The new status symbol is an athletic body in a designer outfit: the stylish radiation of professional, mental and physical success. Out of fashion is the sweaty, worn-out look. We yearn for luxury, sexy styling and rich fabric on the streets, on the beach and in the gym. Fashion brands, always on high alert for consumer trends, got the message loud and clear, and translated it smoothly into a wide range of irresistible must-haves. Chanel golf balls and Kenzo surf boards are designed to make us addicts. Top designers sign up for unique partnerships within fashion and sportswear. Sporty clothing goes for a stylish look these days. The crossover is very obvious from both sides.'

This leads us to the fashion world of today, where anything is possible. Collaborations between sportswear and high fashion are widely discussed on the internet. Online brands are emerging and booming on the net. Is this the trend for the next few years? The internet increasingly shares our lives. We order our clothes online with Zalando, pick our fitness partners on Facebook, and find a fitness centre with one click on the net, we look at our

Huawei or I-watch to measure our heart rate per mile. Sport becomes a choice because we have so many things to do. Motivation to do sports is important. Stylish, comfy or cool sport outfits help to motivate us to do sports. Sportswear, street wear and Haute Couture have now united thanks to the direction and vision of their creative directors. Designers and fashion houses have opened up to a wide variety of influences. This new direction has propelled fashion into new and ground breaking areas. The publicity and press from fashion magazines have been key in this new bold direction.

© Sara De Graeve

# AMERICA'S LEGACY IN SPORTSWEAR

**Sportswear is seen as America's legacy in the history of fashion design.** European designers have been amazed by the incredible success story of American sportswear. Sportswear started as the casual style of American women in the 1920s. The motto back then was, 'Get rid of the long dresses from Europe that made sports such as cycling, tennis and swimming impossible! Let's dress ourselves!'

# Do not forget sportswear, remember it.

Americans wanted to reinvent fashion and succeeded in doing so. Women in the roaring Twenties were searching for new clothes to liberate them and embraced the ease and style of comfortable skirts, light blouses, shirts and colourful shorts. Comfortable, casual and practical clothes had to meet the demands of the fashion-conscious man and woman rejecting tradition and old restrictions in fashion.

Sportswear first made its appearance in the wardrobes of elite men and women of the 20th Century. The origin of sportswear is in the wardrobes of dandies and fashion-lovers-avant-la-lettre. Golf knickers, tennis outfits and swimwear became their go-to-outfits. The meaning of sportswear widened in the 1930s in terms of the appropriate moment to wear items, and the notion of formality.

The Second World War was a milestone in the history of casual wear and sportswear. Women went into service and wore military uniforms. Clothes became more practical, and trousers became accepted in a woman's wardrobe. The fashion industry in the United States changed completely and differed from the fashion industry in France. The style was 'American Sportswear'. American designers such as Claire McCardell (1905-1958) and

Norman Norell became trendsetters when they worked for Hattie Carnegie (1889-1956) who launched 'spectator sportswear'.

**Hattie Carnegie** is a monumental figure in American fashion. Carnegie was the first to introduce ready-to-wear to the high-end market. She used her experience as a milliner to start up a very successful shop on East 10th Street in New York, named Carnegie – Ladies' Hater, where she sold couture from Paris. Her career peaked when she designed the Women's Army Corps (WAC) uniform in 1950 and launched the Popover dress for lady swimmers, and ballet slippers for women who were not doing ballet.

**Claire McCardell** created the 'American Look', a democratic and casual approach to fashion rejecting the formality of French couture. She is considered to be a pioneer in the use of the bias cut, which she incorporated into her own work. Her clothes were very much American: functional, cheap and stylish even if they were part of mass-production. Mass-production in the fashion industry was a consequence of The Great Depression when people sought more comfortable and cheaper clothes.

**Norman Norell (1900-1972)** was hired by Hattie Carnegie in 1928. The simplicity and quality of his elegant suits and tailored silhouettes were his trademark.

These three American designers became legendary in the States and set the precedent for mass-produced ready-to-wear clothing. The leading names in American sportswear design in the 1930s were Tom Brigance and Clare Potter.

Hollywood overtook Paris' role as the style capital of the world and dictated the fashions of the time. Hollywood stars such as James Dean and Natalie Wood in *Rebel without a Cause* (1955) launched the trend of denim pants and T-shirts for men and checkered dresses with a high line above the hips for girls. James Dean's influence on streetwear and on our clothes today is undeniable. Dean is an icon in fashion who became famous for his sportive looks. Vivienne Westwood incorporated his biker jacket look and named the black leather jacket 'the perfecto'; the perfect cool jacket for men and women. James Dean is more than a fashion icon because his clothes live on in wardrobes where they may make a comeback.

The outfits of students at American universities in the 1950s along with the surf and skate cultures of the West Coast made our men and women look and feel sporty. Denim, T-shirts, baseball caps and sneakers were all a part of this look. Comfort is the trademark of both sportswear and street wear. Local surfboard designer Shawn Stussy sold printed T-shirts and then expanded his sales to boutiques. Jack O'Neill discovered the need of swimwear on the West Coast and designed his first wetsuit for surfers.

The younger generation of the 1960s rejected their parents fashion and wore mini-dresses, unisex clothes and panties. Fashion during the Swinging Sixties was influenced by the democratisation of style around the world.

© Keystone_France/Gamma Rapho

The successful American mission to the moon, and the trip into space by Russian cosmonaut Yuri Gagarin, inspired French designers. André Courrèges, Emanuel Ungaro, Pierre Cardin and Paco Rabanne launched futuristic fashion using new synthetic materials from sportswear and abstract designs for mini-dresses with helmets, or long straight dresses with low arm openings.

Couturiers such as Yves Saint Laurent gave clients the chance to buy his clothes at a cheaper price with the launch of

his ready-to-wear line SAINT LAURENT Rive Gauche. *Prêt-à-porter* became the most important fashion product of the Sixties. Clothes became available in standard sizes and were sold
directly to the consumer in the supermarket or in shops belonging to the designer.

During the seventies, Haute Couture became old-fashioned and suffered following the
retirement of Balenciaga and the death of fashion legend Coco Chanel. Milan emerged as
the new fashion centre, with brands such as Prada, Gucci and Fendi. Armani started his
own company and reinvented the men's suit. Italians were pioneers in sportswear with
resounding names such as Emilio Pucci, Simonetta Visconti and Ottavio Missoni, who
sought comfort and sophistication.

The Italian designers were the first to work together on a wider scale than the Americans.

American fashion legend and hat designer Roy Halston paved the way for the introduction of a new sports fashion with his practical clothes for the modern woman, especially
the launch of his shirt dress. Calvin Klein continued this tradition of casual clothes in the
1980s using colours such as beige, cream and grey. His marketing campaign in the nineties,
introducing very young models such as Kate Moss, was the start of a new revolution in
fashion.

Sports brands such as Nike were booming in the 1980s with the introduction of their
magical sports shoes that made giant Adidas envy the sudden rise of the American newcom-
er. Using Nike air technology combined with the endorsement of famous basketball player,
Michael Jordan, was a marketing strategy that worked. Run DMC's collaboration with Adidas did not stop Nike's rise to power.

The 1990s had its own grunge style, influenced by Seattle bands Pearl Jam and Nirvana.
Oversized flannel shirts, worn denim, vintage flower dresses and sturdy boots were the uniform of the grunge boy or girl. Marc Jacobs, Ralph Lauren and Anna Sui copied the trend in
various collections and were inspired by grunge style. Ralph Lauren started his grunge-in-
spired line 'Supply and Denim' in 2011 and created the uniforms for the American team for
the opening and closing ceremonies of the Winter Olympic Games in 2014. He added an
American touch to these uniforms with the slogans 'Land of the Free' and 'Home of the
Brave' in the jackets and shoes of the athletes. British designer Stella McCartney did the
same for Great Britain and was the first designer to make clothes for all sports disciplines

during the 2012 London Olympic Games. Today she is a household name in the competitive and ever-changing world of sportswear. Stella is unique because she was the first woman at the top of the sports industry.

Stijn Helsen is Belgium's best tailor and costume designer. In 2012 he was asked to make the official outfits for the Belgian Olympic team at the London Games. With his Savile Row style, he wanted the garments to fit the athletic body. Every outfit was made individually for 370 participants, including Olympic and Paralympic athletes and coaches. Helsen's job as outfitter of the Belgian team made him excel in tailoring. He did all the fittings and the clothes were made to measure, which is important if you take into consideration the small waists, strong shoulders and muscled legs of the athletes. Helsen looks back happily on the job and reflects on the history of sportswear. 'In the old days, people went hunting, fly fishing and played golf and tennis in posh, tailor-made linen clothes. This changed when people started to look for comfort. Now we see the opposite happening. Stars and rappers wear sportswear and caps to go out, or to go dining.'

Today, ready-to-wear has become accessible to everyone and has incorporated elements of Haute Couture and sportswear. This is the secret success formula for brands such as H&M and Zara. Both European labels have recently introduced a sports collection. Contemporary sportswear is much more than just activewear designed for participants in sports. Sportswear requires a lot. The professional or amateur sportsman or woman wants comfort and is looking for clothes to keep him or her warm in winter or to cool off in the summertime. Designers want clothes to absorb sweat and they find this in spandex, a material especially designed for the world of sports. A sportswoman does not want heavy clothes, but prefers light material for her sports outfit because this allows her to move more easily and rapidly.

# SPORTSWEAR IS BIG BUSINESS

**Sport is big business.** Therefore sportswear is big business too. Football is one of the most popular sporting games in the world. In the US, basketball and American football rule the sports scene. In Europe and South America football is the number one sport. The national and professional league teams in England, Spain, Italy, France and Germany inspire the whole world. Wales, Iceland, Holland and Belgium may be small nations, but become huge on the field. No other games are so widely watched as the FA Cup, the FIFA World Cup and

© Adidas

the Champions League. International brands focus enormously on football. Football apparel is a commercial success that inspires others. Dutch brand COPA has a whole range of T-shirts and recycled bags made from old shirts from a variety of football teams. COPA launched retro outfits from the Fifa World Cup teams. COPA is also the sponsor of the Tibetan team; this shows how international and even political football and sponsorship have become.

Sponsorship is another business venture involving sporting brands. Sponsorship in the world of football involves dazzling amounts of money. Image rights for a famous football player can cost 50% more than their transfer value. David Beckham was the first player whose popularity as a soccer player excelled his sporting exploits on the field. The earnings of the English football player at the end of his career were extraordinary and may set the tone for generations of football players with the same aspirations. This generation is upon us. Expensive transfer fees are headline news.

Why is sponsorship such big business? Well, when you are a football fan you want to wear your idol's shirt. What parent does not want to see his/her toddler in the colours and stripes of their favourite team? This proves that sportswear is more than a matter of comfort, functionality and trends. Adidas and Puma show that there is more to sportswear than the the player's shirt. There is also his body. The underlying message to men is: let's show off your muscular and toned physique. Don't forget to wear your shirt if you want to impress someone. And female football players? We barely know the names of any internationally successful female football players. How about other famous sportswomen? The world of tennis is most accessible to female sports superstars. In other sports, Allyson Felix is America's top female runner. She personifies the successful sportswoman who has a killer body and a great sense of style. Jordanian/Dubai princess Haya Bint al-hussein said on the Dutch blog Glamourland that the sport with the most equality between men and women is horse racing. Women jockeys are as important as their male counterparts.

The outrageous success of sports stars is a fact because they are judged both on and off the sports field. Their sense of style is a widely discussed topic. This rule applies to all sports stars with celebrity status. We pay special attention to celebrities because they often show off new items. No wonder people love them.

# LEADING SPORTS

Brands

# Designers

# BASKETBALL

**How American can a sport be?** Basketball is a true American invention and enormously popular in the States. Every sports lover around the world knows the NBA competition. The National Basketball Association is one of the most powerful sports associations from the East to the West Coast of the States. Basketball has an enormous influence today that is a far cry from its early days. Basketball players are the true giants of sportswear. Quite literally too, think of giants of the game such as Michael Jordan and Magic Johnson, who became internationally recognised for their talent on the sports field and their glamorous lifestyle. Their fame is far greater than the fame of the first basketball players at the International Young Men's Christian Association Training School in Springfield, who were trained in 1891 by the Canadian-American trainer and instructor Dr. James Naismith. He sought a vigorous indoor game to keep his students occupied and at proper levels of fitness during the long New England winters. He also wrote the basic rules and used a peach basket. Today, this peach basket has become a hoop and open net, which was not the case in its early days. The players had to retrieve the balls manually after each 'basket' or point scored. Basketball is played by two teams of five players on a rectangular court. A team can score by shooting the ball through the basket.

You can score two points if a player is closer to the basket than the three-point line, and three points if the player is behind the three-point line. The team with the most points at the end of the game wins, but overtime may be given when the game ends with a draw. 'Dribbling' means advancing the ball on the court by bouncing it while walking or running or throwing it to a team mate. It is a violation to move without dribbling the ball, to carry it, or to hold

© Patrizia Pepe

the ball with both hands then resume dribbling. Retired Belgian Olympic basketball player and rower Yves Defraigne says rules and fouls belong to the game of basketball. He adds: 'Viewers with no knowledge of basketball may have questions about the game. Basketball is a defensive and offensive game that requires teamwork. Defence and attack follow each other. A basketball player can score fast, unlike a football player. This makes basketball exciting.' Every player has a role in the game, from the tallest members of a team, to shorter players with the best ball-handling skills.

**How did Nike become the global leader in sportswear?** Nike started off as a pioneer in athletic footwear that would redefine the industry. The story of the company includes three men. Bill Bowerman was a nationally respected track and field coach at the University of Oregon, who experimented with different track surfaces, re-hydration drinks and in-

novations in running shoes. Bowerman began cobbling shoes together with Phil Knight, a talented middle-distance runner from Portland, who called Onitsuka Co. in Japan, and persuaded the manufacturer of Tiger shoes to make Knight a distributor of Tiger running shoes in the United States. Knight sent several pairs to Bowerman and offered to become his partner, who provided his footwear design ideas to Tiger.

Johnson became the first full-time employee in 1965, and quickly became an invaluable utility man for the start-up company. Johnson did the marketing, established a mail-order system, opened the first BRS retail store (located in Santa Monica, Calif.) and managed shipping/receiving. He also designed several early Nike shoes,

© Nike

and conjured up the name Nike in 1971. Knight and Bowerman started manufacturing their own brand of athletic shoes called 'Swoosh'. The Nike line of footwear debuted in 1972 with sole that had waffle-type nubs for traction and were lighter than traditional training shoes.

With a new logo, a new name and a new design innovation, runner Steve Prefontaine joined the company and became the 'soul of Nike'. The 1980s were a decade of transition and redirection for Nike. Nike entered the 1980s on a roll thanks to the successful launch of Nike Air technology in the Tailwind running shoe in 1979. By the end of 1980, Nike

© Nike

completed its IPO and became a publicly traded company. The debut of a new signature shoe for NBA star Michael Jordan in 1985 helped bolster Nike's bottom line.

By the end of the decade, Nike had regained its position as the industry leader; the first and only time a company in the athletic footwear/apparel industry accomplished such a feat. Nike has never relinquished that position since. During the 1990s Nike extended its reach and started to expand further.

Encouraged by a series of successful product launches and marketing campaigns, Nike entered the 1990s by christening its world headquarters in suburban Portland, Oregon.

While Nike had designed footwear and apparel for golf and soccer for a number of years, the mid-1990s signalled a deepening commitment to truly excel in these sports. In 1994, Nike signed several individual players from what would become the World Cup-winning Brazilian National Team and also signed the US men's and women's national soccer teams, as well as dozens of national teams from around the world.

In 1996, Nike Golf landed the vastly talented young golfer 'Tiger' Woods for a reported $5 million per year. Nike rang in the new millennium with a new footwear cushioning system called Nike Shox, which debuted during the Sydney Olympic Games in 2000. With more than 15 years of perseverance and dedication, Nike designers stuck with their idea until technology could catch up. The result was a cushioning and stability system worthy of joining Nike Air as the industry's gold standard in sports footwear.

Just as Nike's products have evolved, so has Nike's approach to marketing. Departing from the traditional 'big athlete, big ad, big product' formula, Nike created a multi-faceted consumer experience in support of the World Cup. 'Secret Tournament' incorporated advertising, the Internet, public relations, retail and consumer events to create excitement for Nike's soccer products and athletes. These days, Nike continues to seek new and innovative ways to develop superior athletic products, and creative methods to communicate directly with consumers. Nike is now also famous for its artistic collaborations with designers such as Riccardo Tisci and Chitose Abe. In his 2015 memoir, *Shoe Dog*, Nike founder and board chairman Phil Knight shared the inside story of the company's early days as an intrepid start-up, and its evolution into one of the world's most iconic, game-changing and profitable brands.

# Patrizia Bambi
## (Patrizia Pepe)

Patrizia Bambi, designer and founder of the Italian brand Patrizia Pepe gives her point of view of sports in terms of high-fashion, casual and sportswear:

'Sportswear has influenced fashion throughout history, but over the past few seasons it has shown an astonishing evolution. Iconic trainers, high-tech fabrics, lycra or scuba details – these are now inevitable elements that give a twist to high-end and casual fashion worldwide. The key word is "gym-on-the-go": refined, chic, sexy, comfortable, and therefore the perfect mix for a super stylish look. The trend highlights sportswear elements, revolutionising the concept of fitness thanks to high-performance yet stylish pieces. And that's exactly what I do in my collections – I'm always inspired by sporty/functional influences. As a gym enthusiast, as well as a fashion designer, I really love collaborations between both sports and fashion industries; a lucky mash-up where style gets sporty – perfect for fit fashionistas.'

Patrizia talks about the importance of sports for her label: 'Patrizia Pepe is a versatile brand, designed for glamorous, confident and dynamic women who love mixing different styles in a personal and effortless way. This is why I always include sporty garments in my collections; whether it be a basketball inspired tank top, an ultralight down jacket or a pair of super-comfy sneakers, reinvented with that unique touch of refinement and detail that always influences my creative approach. It is vital to capture and mirror contemporary trends, and over the last decades active wear and athletic apparel has undoubtedly come to play a major role in the fashion world. Sportswear is really important as it has the power to be interpreted in a casual way and recharged with unexpected shades, graphic patterns and shiny embellishments. It's more about an attitude than a category of clothes. You can see this clearly in urban sportswear, where timeless silhouettes taken from the athletic world, such as sweatshirts and leggings, are reinvented with splashes of colour, appealing prints and couture inlays.'

© Patrizia Pepe

Patrizia Bambi also sees the evolution of sportswear from the streets to the catwalk. 'I like the way something purely minimal is transformed with a hip, sophisticated mood. This is exactly what happened when sportswear made its appearance in runway shows, starting in the '80s and ending up with today's increasing demand for easy-to-wear, alluring essentials. Sporty chic is a central trend that perfectly conveys the fast-paced lifestyle of contemporary women.

And in this new era of street-style fashion, the evolution of sportswear is literally exploding into a fantastic, creative freedom of mixing and matching different materials and textures in ways we have never seen before, reminiscent of college team uniforms and downtown playing fields.'

Where does Patrizia's love for sportswear come from? 'I love sportswear! I am an "on the move" kind of woman, both at work

© Patrizia Pepe

and play, and this is definitely reflected in the way I dress. From early morning at the office to evening with my friends, I like wearing clothes that make me feel feminine, yet always comfortable. Be it a basic T-shirt over a pair of riding pants for a day-time look, or a gym-inspired jumpsuit with stiletto heels at night.'

Finally, Patrizia tells us a revealing story: 'A famous swimming champion once said:

"You can't put a limit on anything. The more you dream, the further you get". I infuse the same philosophy into my job and my life and I will definitely continue to do so.'

# RUNNING

**On a sunny Sunday in Paris,** I wondered why so many men and women took to running the streets. I asked a male runner in the park around the Louvre what sportswear and style meant to him and he replied, 'that doing sport is magic and that sportswear is the magic wand.' He continued, 'Sport keeps you in shape and it makes you feel good. Sportswear makes you feel even better. This is important to realise as you become your own personal trainer where the quality of running matters.'

Running is probably the oldest sport known to man. Every hunter in prehistoric times knew how to run. Running helped hunters to catch their prey or was a life-saving activity when

© Adidas

## Doing sport is magic and sportswear is the magic wand

the hunter's life was in danger. Mankind and animals knew how to run. This explains why every parent is proud of their baby when he takes his first steps.

We have come so far from this. Nowadays running is regarded as a notable sports discipline, with top female athletes Allyson Felix, Paula Radcliffe, Almaz Ayana, Dafne Schippers and male runner Usain Bolt, nicknamed 'Lightning Bolt' or 'Gold Bolt' because of his great speed. He was the first athlete to win the Olympic Gold Medal for the 100 m distance three times in a row and to win the triple triple in Rio in 2016.

Running is very popular because everyone can run. You only need the right footwear. Good shoes are essential for running. The right pair of shoes makes you fly over the running track. Talking about sports shoes, almost makes us forget about a good pair of socks, a T-shirt and a track suit or shorts.

Running is so popular because it frees our mind and it releases endorphins in our brain. A female barrister told me that she runs at least 3 times a week. She says: 'I love running, because it makes me forget the difficult cases I deal with and I often find solutions while running. It is pure liberation of the mind and it's good for the body. It is the secret to a "body and soul in harmony". She also pointed out the danger of exaggerating our effort to run too far too soon. She explains: 'Give your body time to adapt to your performance. Don't stress your body. This will only cause injuries and will make you give up running.'

© Adidas

Don't stress
your body

Running differs from walking in the sense that we move rapidly on foot. Competitive racing brings us back to the Taliteann Games in Ireland almost 2000 years ago. The Olympic Games introduced running in 776 BC. Today, running has never been so popular and widespread as a sporting activity. A male runner who ran marathons all over the world, from New York to Berlin, explains why running is so important: 'Running is good for my body and is like the ideal wake-up call for my body. It activates my body and keeps me fit. It takes discipline to run and I have a goal. Thanks to running I learn to set myself a goal and shift my boundaries. My body looks better as a runner and running is the most effective sport. Yes, I am happy to be a runner! For me, this is going *back to basics*. My body needs resilience, endurance, balance and coordination. It does not feel like running or doing sports, it completely overwhelms me.'

PUMA originates in sport and ends in fashion. PUMA is one of the world's leading sport lifestyle companies that designs and develops footwear, apparel and accessories. Puma's Sport performance and lifestyle labels include categories such as Football, Running, Motorsports, Golf, and Sailing. The 'Black Label' features collaborations with renowned designer labels such as Alexander McQueen, Yasuhiro Mihara and Sergio Rossi. Puma's sponsorships are deals that are the envy of the other giants. The effect of the Puma logo on the minds of sportsmen is also something that many marketing departments may

© Puma

wonder about. Puma has a positive image. It is committed to working in ways that contribute to the world by supporting creativity, sustainability and peace, and by staying true to the principles of being fair, honest, positive and creative in making decisions. PUMA has taken the world of sports by storm since its beginnings in 1948 when Rudolf Dassler launched his own successful brand PUMA. Puma is the brainchild of Rudolf Dassler, one of the Dassler brothers who both started a sportwear giant. The story of Adi and Rudolf Dassler is unique in the world of sportswear. Both Bavarian brothers had worked in the family business Die Gebrüder Dassler Sportschuhfabrik until a feud after the Second World War caused a rift in the company and both decided to start up their own label. The handy and introvert Adi Dassler created the company which later became the successful

© Puma

label Adidas, while the more extrovert Rudolf Dassler created Puma in 1948. More than 60 years later, Puma has become one of the big players in sportswear with a big tradition in sponsoring events/sportsclubs and collaborations with sportsmen such as Ibrahim Afellay, Yaya Touré and Marco Reus and celebrities such as Rihanna.

Puma sponsored the greatest football players Pele, Eusebio, Cruyff and Maradona, and Puma teams won several World Cups in Puma outfits. In 2008, Usain Bolt broke the 100 meter world record in 9.69 seconds and in 2009 Bolt broke his own record and reduced his time to 9.58 seconds. Usain Bolt won 3 times at the London Olympic games and did the same in Rio in 2016.

The Football World Cup or European Championship are the ideal platforms to show Puma's latest innovations. The introduction of new Puma shoes has always been a special event to sportsmen: think of the Puma 'ATOM' (1948), the Super ATOM shoe launched in 1960, followed by the Torero Boot (designed for Maradona) in 1982, the Puma Disc, which was the first laceless sports shoe, or the Mostro, the mix of a sprint-spike and surfing shoe. The Speed Boot V 1.06 (launched after the Millennium) was the world's lightest football boot.

The PUMA Group owns the brands PUMA, Cobra Golf and Tretorn. The company, an example of the German *Wirtschaftswunder,* distributes its products in more than 120 countries, employs more than 11,000 people worldwide and has headquarters in Germany, Boston, London and Hong Kong. Puma has partnerships with Ferrari, Ducati and BMW to make Puma-Ferrari, Puma-Ducati and Puma-BMW shoes. Since the beginning, young people have adored the brand and are part of the hype of the PUMA enterprise. PUMA is very trendy, can make a comeback anytime, and can be the hottest label.

# Puma can make a comeback anytime

# Stella McCartney

Stella McCartney's imprint on sportswear for women is obvious and she will therefore be recognised as a prolific innovator of high fashion and sportswear. Her legacy will show that she discovered the need for women to dress as well as men while doing sports. Sporty women at the turn of the century were not getting the attention they deserved and Stella McCartney did something about it. She was discovered by Adidas in 2002. This was the start of a fascinating collaboration that grew and turned into fashion's most successful marriage between high street fashion and sports. Stella McCartney explains how it all started: 'I collaborated with Adidas once before in 2002 on a pair of limited edition sneakers. We stayed in touch and they proposed that we work on a performance line for women together, as I felt it had always been an ill-addressed area. Working with Adidas is a lifetime opportunity to give female sports enthusiasts a choice.'

Shortly after the turn of the century, Stella McCartney was given her own line of sportswear alongside her own very successful fashion label and was the first woman in fashion to do so. Were women not given the same respect that men got in the world of sports? Stella answers: 'I felt like there was nothing for women who wanted to look good while they worked out. And I always had a feeling the women's category was being taken less seriously than men's, and that we weren't getting the technology or design we deserved.'

Technology opened up a whole new world for modern women who were driven into the gym, the park, the streets. Feeling sexy in the world of sports, McCartney explains, was something new. 'It's very similar to where I find inspiration for all the other things I do normally. It's mostly being inspired by real women, naturally sexy modern women, so I try to get into their heads and figure out their needs. These needs are obviously very different when it comes to sports performance, but I try to use the normal inspirations that I look at… film, music, everyday life really.'

The joy Stella receives from this work is her compelling drive to inspire more women into sports. Her message to women is clear. 'I really wanted to encourage women to get more involved in sports, because there's a real strength to that. With this range I wanted to celebrate life, fitness and health. It's not the easiest thing in the world to keep fit, and in everyone's busy lives to find the time to stay healthy and work out. So I want to encourage it by making sportswear inviting and desirable – trying to inject colour, life and energy – and fashion.'

There is no particular item she loves most. 'There are so many pieces that I love, I wear all of it!'

# FOOTBALL

**Are men and football a match?** Football is the world's biggest sport in terms of sponsorship, transfer money and profit for professional clubs. Everyone knows the teams of Real Madrid, AC Milan, Chelsea and PSG. Football has its big events. We all want to be present at the World Cup Football, the Champions League and the European Football Cup. The English FA Cup is the oldest in the world. In Europe, football is the number one sport. In England alone, there are 92 professional clubs and the 5 London clubs are respected internationally as top clubs. The London top clubs are Arsenal and Chelsea. London, Madrid and Paris attract talent and pay well. Their status is that of a superstar. The players almost make us forget the game. At the centre of every match is the football game between two teams of eleven players who want to score goals. In order to score, the football player needs to control the ball and put it in the opposition's goal. The keeper's task is to prevent this from happening.

Control of the ball is essential for both sets of players as well as for the keepers. Football is a powerful game. Football is suspense. No wonder football is a global business. Market leaders Nike, Adidas and Puma have the status of giants of sportswear thanks to football. Football legends Cruyff, Pele, Best and Maradona

© Puma

have become immortal thanks to their exploits on the field. Our love of football is like a religion and watching a football match is like attending a church service. According to Belgian personal trainer and ex-professional football player for AA Gent, André Raes: 'Every boy dreams of a professional career as football player, but he forgets that it takes much training and discipline to become an excellent player. The attraction of football lies in the special atmosphere that creates victory and defeat, the support of your fans and the world around football. Euphoria on the field may quickly change into a feeling of defeat. It often happens that a favourite team is out of the game and that the underdog wins the cup. It takes a lot to grow as a team and work on your weak passes. A good trainer is a true leader who inspires and motivates his team. He is a man with charisma. Here's my advice to every football player: stay down-to-earth and show that sport is all about fun! There is no better medicine for stress or misery than a good game of football between two great teams. The million viewers of the World Cup and other cups prove this.'

© Shutterstock

**ADIDAS was founded by Adolf Dassler on 18 August 1949** and was named after its founder. However, turbulent struggles between the two Dassler brothers were to define German sportswear. Adidas became Adolf Dassler's company and his brother Rudolf launched Puma after a feud between the two brothers. Adi Dassler tells how it all began: 'I grew up in a working class family. We weren't poor, but we were awfully close. I started designing and making my first sports shoes in the laundry room of my parents home. Business is never easy, even when working with family.'

Where did Adidas founder Adi Dassler's love of sportswear come from? He once said: 'I love sports. I have loved them all my life and I knew there was a better way to equip the athletes. I understood that equipment can help an athlete perform better. There are things I could make that would help athletes keep their footing in wet weather. That is how the idea for spikes on shoes came about. I had to try all my shoes myself to make sure they worked right.' Adidas became a record holder in patents in sportswear. About his other invention, the three famous stripes, he says: 'The three stripes were originally installed on the shoes to give that part of the shoe more support, but it became our trademark.'

© Adidas

The guiding principle of Adidas 'sport performance' is 'Play to Win'. Inspired by the motivation of founder Adi Dassler, 'sport performance' brings passion for great products to athletes in all sports, allowing them to be faster, stronger, smarter, cooler and natural. The main focus of Adidas' 'sport performance' label is on five key categories: football, basketball, running, training and outdoor. The fashion group owned by Adidas is defined as the future of sportswear and includes the labels Y-3, Porsche Design Sport, Adidas SLVR and Adidas NEO. Through these four labels Adidas brings authentic sportswear to the full spectrum of lifestyle consumers. Famous creative forces such as Stella McCartney, Mary Karantzou and Yohij Yamamoto have given the brand more glamour and better design, The first athlete to wear Adidas shoes was the American runner Jesse Owens in 1936. In 1954, the German team competed against Hungary and won, wearing soccer boots that featured removable studs for the first time. During the 1960s, Adidas manufactured

© Adidas

equipment for what some consider 'fringe sports' driven by a desire to help all athletes committed to performance.

Unconventional high jumper Dick Fosbury launched himself up and over in Adidas footwear. The Adidas-wearing German football team, with Franz Beckenbauer, brought glory to Adidas during the World Cup when Germany beat Holland 2-1 in the 1974 final. During the 1980s the story of a successful family business continued as Adi's wife Käthe, his son Horst, and his daughters carried on the business after founder Adi Dassler's death in 1978. Adidas is known today as a very successful family business turned into a major multinational. Under the CEO Robert Louis-Dreyfus in the 1990s, Adidas moved from being a manufacturing and sales based company to a marketing company. In 1995, Adidas entered the Frankfurt and Paris Stock Exchanges. 1996 was a lucrative year for the company as the 'three-stripes company' equipped 6,000 Olympic athletes from 33 countries. Athletes wearing the three stripes won 220 medals, including 70 gold. Apparel sales increased by 50%. Following personnel changes, the new management initiated an ambitious 'growth and efficiency programme'. In 2013 Adidas changed running forever with its focus on quality through revolutionary energy return, superior cushioning, optimal fit and temperature independence. Adidas introduced the 'Energy Boost' – a cushioning technology that provided the highest energy return in the running industry. And just like that, running will never be the same again. Adidas is clearly more than just a brand aiming at men, women and children who 'play to win'... but dresses those who want to remain stylish for sports.

# Ermanno Daelli

## (Ermanno Scervino)

Mr Ermanno Daelli, of the brand Ermanno Scervino, is the outfitter of the Italian national football team. He started the luxury brand with his partner Scervino in 2000. How did he become involved in sportswear? 'I have always found it interesting to work on sportswear. I like to make sportier materials interact with handcrafted techniques. In my opinion, the result is a high-quality product, which at the same time is absolutely modern. For my brand, therefore, it has been a very natural decision to start partnerships with the world of sports. The first partnership was with the Russian national team (Olympic Winter Games, Turin 2006), and then with the Azerbaijan national team (Olympic Games, London 2012, and the European Games, Baku 2005). Finally, still in 2015, we became "luxury partner" of FIGC, designing the uniforms for the Italian football team until 2018.'

Mr Daelli is obviously excited about being the outfitter for the Italian team. 'Yes, I am very proud of this job. The national football team is the symbol of Italian character all over the world, and we are honoured to dress them in our 100% Made In Italy symbol: Michelangelo's David. I found this triangulation between Italian excellence really emotional.'

What does he think is important as a designer of sportswear? 'The base, in my opinion, is always the material, where quality guarantees a high-quality final product. However, materials alone are not sufficient – they have to be processed with craftsmanship and know-how, which represent the essence of the brand. In the near future we will continue to be the "luxury partner" of the Italian football team until the 2018 Word Cup in Russia. Then we will be happy to evaluate new interesting opportunities.'

ERMANNO SCERVINO

ERMANNO SCERVINO

© Courtesy of Ermanno Scervino

# TENNIS

**Do you remember Serena, Novak, Rafael and Roger?**
No need to mention their surnames, we all know these tennis
stars. Tennis has two faces: it is the sport of global tennis stars,
but also of the amateur players finding enjoyment in tennis.

Tennis matches have become international events and outgrown their origins as *jeux de paume* at the French court, or
a simple game with a ball and a racket, played later in the
gardens of English mansions. Watching a tennis match
on TV or in a club is almost as exciting as playing one
yourself. Tennis is entertainment. Tennis is a show.
Tennis is more than just working out or a game. It
is exciting for both tennis players and spectators.
Tennis is a sport with many fans, from the recreational tennis players in their tennis clubs who
meet every weekend, to the professional stars
who take tennis to its highest level.

An eighteen-year old girl who has played
tennis since she was a child and is now a
children's coach explains: 'Tennis is a sport
that you play with two players. This is an

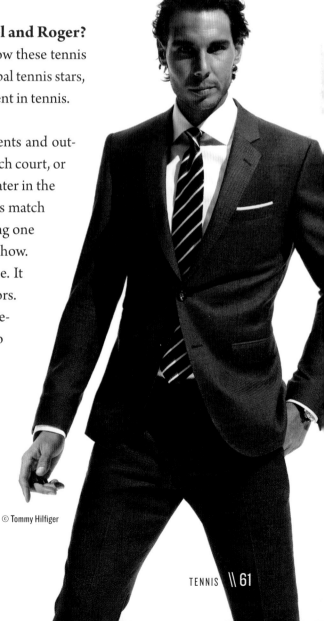

© Tommy Hilfiger

© Hackett

advantage compared to a football team of eleven players where all members of the team need to be present in order to play the game. And indeed, tennis is all about the game! Anyone can play a match at his or her level and enjoy playing tennis. There is a kind of competition from the very start, which is motivating to most players.

Tennis can be played throughout the whole year: outdoors in spring and summer and indoors in the autumn and winter. Many people love tennis because it is a social sport where many social contacts are established. Tennis is all about coordination and technique. It is a sport for all ages and star players are part of tennis.'

The idea of stepping onto a tennis court without stockings, petticoats and long sleeves came from the French champion Suzanne Lenglen in the 1920s, who had been hired by French designer Jean Patou as director of the sportswear department. The 1930s still forced women to wear longer skirts, which made it difficult for them to play their game. Gussie Moran or 'Gorgeous Gussie' caused a revolution in 1949 when she appeared on a Wimbledon court in a short white dress.

Star players such as the Frenchman René Lacoste, Englishman Fred Perry, and Swede Björn Borg have outgrown their status as sporting heroes and all started second careers as designers of tennis clothes. Tennis outfits have always been very modish in style, a look that attracted great international sales. Fred Perry launched his Fred Perry shirts with an embroidered laurel-wreath insignia and is now a leader of street wear in the United Kingdom and across the world. His Fred Perry branded shirts were already being worn by the London subculture of the 1960s – the Mods. Today's Fred Perry is Swedish tennis player Björn Borg.

# BJÖRN BORG

**Thank you Björn!** Thanks to the Swedish tennis star Borg, tennis changed from being 'a white sport' into a colourful scene for the passionate and the active. Conservatism and conformism in sports came to an end with Björn Borg, who showed the world that being active and making a difference is far more attractive than playing it safe. It is this attitude that is the core of the Björn Borg brand.

© Jimmy Backius

That is how fashion is created and how people should wear it. Björn Borg started the Swedish fashion company that makes products designed to 'make you look and feel active and attractive'. Björn Borg takes pride in providing the best comfort and fit for the colourful and the brave. Björn Borg's core business is underwear but the company also offers sportswear and fragrances as well as footwear, luggage and bags and eyewear through licensees. Björn Borg has been listed on the NASDAQ since 2007.

The brand Björn Borg became a household name in the 1990s for sportswear and for its colourful underwear. The name Björn Borg is a resounding name in tennis. Björn Borg was the

© Keystone-France/Gamma Rapho

first tennis player to win Wimbledon five times in a row and the French Open six times. Björn Borg won the BBC Sports Personality of the Year – Overseas Personality award in 1979. He became a legend thanks to his winning philosophy. His own words, 'If you are afraid of losing, you daren't win' became meaningful in describing his career on the tennis court and later as fashion mogul.

Björn Borg conquered the world on the tennis court in the 1970s and early 1980s, but now conquers the arena of sporty and fashionable underwear and sportswear. Björn Borg has reinvented sportswear and underwear and the legend himself has worked as a source of inspiration for the company and its products, which were very successful in Scandinavia, then in Europe and now sell all over the world. Björn Borg inherited the spirit of entrepreneurship from his father, who was a salesman. Borg became 'Mr. Cool' on the tennis court and in business. His nicknames 'the Iceman', 'The Iceberg' and 'Iceborg' referred to the fact that Borg showed no emotions on the tennis court but also held the promise of a stern talented tennis player turned businessman. Björn Borg is widely recognised as the world's greatest tennis player in history. His five successive wins at Wimbledon were only equalled by Swiss tennis player Roger Federer. Björn Borg's talent was discovered at a very young age when he won the Junior title at Wimbledon aged fifteen.

Borg's illustrious predecessor Lacoste invented the tennis ball canon to shoot balls to players, the metal tennis racket and polyurethane golf stick. Björn Borg is a resounding name known for its logo, consisting of a tennis ball, and the brand became identified by its flashy colours. Lacoste equally became identified with his logo from 1927 onwards, named after his nickname 'The Crocodile'. The story behind this goes that: René Lacoste admired the crocodile leather suitcase owned by the captain of the French Davis Cup team in 1927, and the latter said: 'If you win, I will buy you one!' Lacoste lost the bet but he was admired by the American press for his performance and they named him 'The Crocodile'.

The lives of Lacoste and Borg show more interesting parallels. Just as Borg's early career had started in the Davis Cup for Sweden, Lacoste's passion for tennis began at the age of 14 and he became a true legend with the renowned 'Mousquetaires' and the Davis Cup Victory in 1927. Lacoste's tenacity and consistency led those around him to compare him to the likes of a Crocodile, never letting go of his prey. Following this, a friend of his drew him an open-mouthed saurian, which René Lacoste quickly stitched onto his white blazer. The signature was born…

The LACOSTE legend was born in 1933, when René Lacoste revolutionised men's fashion, replacing the classical woven fabric, long-sleeved and starched shirts on the courts, with what has now become the classic LACOSTE polo shirt. Almost 80 years after its creation, LACOSTE has become a lifestyle brand, combining elegance and comfort. LACOSTE founds its success on the essential values of authenticity, performance, and elegance. The crocodile today embodies the elegance of the champion.

Björn Borg was equally in search of new, trendy, elegant yet comfortable clothing to replace the classic white tennis shirt traditionally worn on tennis courts. Both realised that there was a demand for new tennis apparel and sportswear.

# James Lee
## (Björn Borg)

Designer James Lee talks passionately about his job at Björn Borg: 'My role at Björn Borg is to set the design directions for the brand each season and to coordinate all the different product groups so that all products from Björn Borg during a season stay true and consistent to a theme and that we end up with a collection that is in line with the brand. It's a great job as it involves so many different products and different ways to bring seasonal ideas, techniques and themes out in them. It's incredibly inspiring to be involved from start to finish and see how the collection takes shape and is realised, presented then sold to the consumers. The role of a designer in a brand like BB is to work with both garments and graphics and innovate within these fields.'

Mr. Lee reveals which elements of sportswear are incorporated in his work: 'We reference sport in different ways; through style, materials and display. There are materials that are inherently sporty, such as rubber, reflectives, synthetic fabrics, plastics, and meshes that, when combined with garnments, produce the BB look, which is a mix of sports and fashion. Styling and garment construction obviously play a big role in this in order to make products with the correct references – both for us as a brand and for the consumer.' Mr Lee explains whom he has in mind when designing: 'We target the colourful and brave; people who are interested in unique garments that make you feel active and attractive. We aim to produce products for people who have a liberated attitude, but are extremely serious about style. The brand's heritage comes from a sports legend, so we naturally have a sports reference and a tendency towards functional and sports lifestyle products. We've been making sportswear since the mid '80s.'

And how stylish should we be? Mr. Lee responds: 'There's a huge amount of stylish sportswear right now. The increasingly close link between sports and fashion means that sportswear is part of street and everyday fashion in new and inspiring ways. This has really blossomed over the past few years, and will be evolving in different ways, as innovations are quickly coming together with an increased cultural focus on health and lifestyle. It is truly inspiring to see and be a part of the development and innovation of this style and how it combines with people's lives.' He describes his job as designer and the requirements of his job: 'We go from the needs of the person who will be using the products. What is the key to perfect comfort, ultimate fit, function, and how do we make the consumer look active and attractive?' Björn Borg as a brand focuses on different sports ranging from running, tennis, training and lifestyle

sports. James Lee jokes about the aspect of colour in the clothes in his brand. 'We believe that people need more colour in their lives! Both men and women!'

James has his own view on sportswear for women and shares it with us: 'Women's sportswear is really important. Women have taken on the trend of wearing sportswear inside and outside the gym more than men have at the moment. Women are really exploring that link between sports and fashion, gym and street in a big way, so this opens up a lot of interesting possibilities for design.'

© Jimmy Backius/Corinna/m4models.de

# I thank Björn Borg
## for my sports bra

© Björn Borg AB

# SKIING

**Skiing is a sport that requires snow.** You glide over snow with long skis attached to boots or shoes on your feet. Or you go snowboarding with just one board attached to your legs. Skiing and the natural environment are one world. A skier who learnt to ski at the age of 5 and who has more than 30 years experience says: 'Skiing is all about technique, coordination, posture, fun and natural surroundings. Skiing is relaxation in the snow and requires great effort from your body. There is always the chance you might fall. So that is why you need to focus on your path on the slopes. The world of skiing is a closed world where everyone knows everyone else. Amateurs admire big stars and stars started off as amateur skiers.'

© Bogner

Until the 19th century, skiing was used for transport in snow-rich areas. Later on, skiing was done for recreation and competition. Competitive classes include slalom, giant slalom, Super-G, downhill or alpine skiing, and disabled skiing. Skiing is now a highly respected olympic sports discipline with many recreational or competitive followers. Every mountain becomes the place to be for the skier. Most skiers practise alpine skiing on slopes in ski resorts in Canada, Switzerland, Italy or France. Scandinavia is the home of skiing. The archeologist Berglund discovered the first ski in a Norse settlement in Greenland, dating back to 1010 BC. Also the word 'ski' has its origins in Scandinavia as it comes on the Old Norse word 'skid' which means 'split piece of wood'. Nordic skiing or cross-country skiing is the oldest form of skiing, using free-heel bindings attached to the toes. Nordic skiing is especially popular in Scandinavia. The Norwegian royals love Nordic skiing and are often photographed skiing. Other celebrities on skis who suffered serious ski accidents include Dutch Royal Prince Friso and Formula 1 star Michael Schumacher, both of whom went off-piste. Does it surprise you that there are more accidents by snowboarders than by skiers?

© Bogner

Skiing is
relaxation
in the snow

Of the most common injuries among skiers, 33% involve the knees, 6.6% the thumb, 6.4% the shoulder, and 2.7% brain concussions. Of the most common injuries among snowboarders, 20.4% involve the wrist, 11.7% the shoulder, 6.2% the ankle and 3.7% brain concussions.

There is at least one comfort for snowboarders: they have a wide choice of all-mountain snowboards. There are real jewels among the snowboards. More accidents can be prevented when you wear a snowboard helmet. Michael Schumacher's helmet proved to be life-saving. Don't think that the helmet can't be elegant! Anon has a beautiful model named 'Blitz' in daring red-purple. The gadget-lover will love the ski helmet 'Receptor BUG' by Dr Dre with a built-in audio system.

For those who like to be stylish in the snow, there is a wide choice of ski apparel. The British designer Jack Frost is *the* brand in snow and ski apparel. So is the brand Eider, which launched its soft cell jacket with hood. When you are up for a real elegant adventure in the snow, look at the collections of established names such as O'Neill, Peak Performance, Bogner, Moncler and Bun. Time to embrace warmth in the freezing cold! From cool snowboarding to ski deluxe, we are truly spoilt for choice. Whether you go skiing in a colourful neon print or in gloomy dark colours, enjoy your ski ride! If you really want to look flashy on the pistes then don't forget your ski sunglasses, or a ski mask to protect you from the mountain sun, snow or fog. Don't skip relaxing après-ski style in the right outfit. Gone is the wet or cold. Just love 'the second skin' aspect of ski apparel. Ski gadgets like these make us dream of Val d'Isère, Val Thorens and Méribel. Every man or woman on skis dreams of après-ski in La Folie Douce before taking dinner in grand style. Who knows, maybe you will glide into a Hollywood star on skis in the snow or afterwards.

© Bogner

## BOGNER

**Bogner is a family-run business in Southern Germany** that has developed into an international company specialising in ski and golf apparel. Company owner, Willy Bogner, is the son of Bavarian parents with a huge interest in ski and fashion. He is one of the few German entrepreneurs in fashion who enjoy a worldwide reputation. Bogner is considered one of the leading international lifestyle brands in ski fashion and sportswear. In addition to his career as a professional athlete, he has also become famous as a film director and producer. For Willy Bogner, who was born in Munich in 1942, all of his occupations have been not only a job, but also a vocation. The alpine skier took part in the Winter Olympics twice (in 1960 and in 1964), won several titles at the German Youth Championship at the age of sixteen and

was the very first German to win the famous 'Lauberhorn Ski Race' at the age of seventeen. He studied economics and clothing engineering and entered the family business in 1972 – 40 years after it was founded in 1932.

© Bogner

In the United States, Bogner learned all he needed to know about running a business. After his father's death in 1977, he returned to Germany to expand the company into one of the most established lifestyle labels in the world. In the late 1960s Willy Bogner devoted himself to another new challenge. In 1968 he founded the film production company 'Willy Bogner Film GMBH' and became

© Bogner

renowned as one of the world's best cameramen on skis. He has worked as a cinematographer, director, actor, producer, and screenwriter, and has taken part in the production of almost 40 movies. Bogner was responsible for the skiing scenes in four James Bond movies, including as cinematographer and director. During his career, his wife Sônia has always encouraged and supported her husband to pursue his dreams.

How do you become a legend in skiwear with a respected name in the business?

'It is the result of a lifelong passion for skiing!', explains Willy Bogner, founder of the German brand BOGNER. 'Skiing is an experience that creates an intense joy. To be in the middle of nature, to float on the snow is a totally different action from walking: it is like flying a plane close to the ground. Thanks to this sport, I have a dream job which is still a great pleasure.' Bogner is a true pioneer in combining sports and creativity. 'I was the first to lead fashion, media, film and shows. I started to film sport events such as the Olympic

Winter Games of Squaw Valley in 1960 as a participant, when filming was not allowed for outsiders. I liked this so much that I continued to film action scenes. Sometimes even on skis. As a professional sportsman, sport has been important on a professional and private level. Bogner brought innovation to sportswear and gained recognition as a brand that stands for sportsmanship, functionality and fashion. The passion for winter sport was always on my mind and on the minds of my parents. My father began as a salesman for skis and knitwear from Norway. My mother, Maria Bogner, came up with the idea of creating ski wear ourselves. Ski wear was often stiff and had a rustic character. There was a need for more functional, modern and stylish ski outfits and my parents revolutionised ski apparel by introducing quality fabrics that stretched. Skiers wanted to move freely and we made this possible! The cuts and models of our outfits were innovative, too. Our wedge pants soon became world famous and were even called 'Bogners' in the States.

The use of stretch-nylon was revolutionary at the time and I was part of this revolution. One year later, I was in charge of the creative and commercial aspects of our ski collections. I always loved creativity.

## Skiers wanted to move freely and we made this possible

— Bogner

This reminds me of the ski musical *Skifascination*, which I filmed with renowned skiers and musicians in 1964. My best cooperation was with stuntman John Eaves with whom I did more than twenty films as cameraman. Later on, producer Albert R. Broccoli asked me to film a sequence on skis for the sixth James Bond film *On Her Majesty's Secret Service*. I first thought that it was a joke to have to carry a camera weighing sixteen kilos while skiing at top speed of eighty km per hour. It is my dream to live out my passion. I admire people who love sports but also have other interests. That is why I create outfits for active people wherever they may be! That is the philosophy of my company, which has luckily continued to grow.'

© Simonetta Ravizza

# Simonetta Ravizza

Skiing is very popular in Italy. Italian designer Simonetta Ravizza explains why: 'We have the beautiful Dolomites mountains near Milan. Our clientele wants to look fabulous and stay warm on their winter vacations. I wanted to make a statement about fashion and sport. Fashion extends to all parts of life and, similarly, sport is equally important. Women want to be active and they want to be fashionable. Therefore, it is important that we combine our resources and collaborate with other sectors to try and meet the needs of the modern woman. Thus the partnership of Simonetta Ravizza and Momo Design, and Simonetta Ravizza and Zero-Ski. It is important to cross thresholds and challenge yourself. The Simonetta Ravizza Skiwear Collection is a capsule collection that was integrated with our Autumn/Winter 2015-2016 collection. It is a unique collection. It was an opportunity to challenge myself and realise a vision of a perfect ski vacation with my family.

The capsule ski collection is for both younger women of around 30 years and the more mature adult woman. It works for both because the collection is timeless and classic.

Design and material are absolutely essential. For skiers and snow enthusiasts of all levels, our skiwear and designer helmets are of the best quality.

The helmets were made in collaboration with Momo Design, another Italian premier brand. The helmets are pure fashion on the outside and pure technical on the inside – a real dual personality!

For our skis that debuted at the Simonetta Ravizza Milan runway show in February 2015, we collaborated with Zero-Ski. Each of those pairs of skis was made by an accomplished team boasting thirty years' experience in the field. Every pair required twelve hours of labour with the work being done in many phases. When you think that normal skis require a production time of about 30 minutes, and then you try the Simonetta Ravizza Zero-Ski skis on the slopes, you will understand the difference! I chose black and white colours for ski wear because of simplicity. Above all, for the understated and chic effect that these colours evoke. They illustrate a sense of timelessness but also modernity – these are constant goals for Simonetta Ravizza.

If you have ever seen the movie *Charade* with Audrey Hepburn and Cary Grant, you will see the type of woman that I was inspired by for my skiwear. At Simonetta Ravizza, I build on my family tradition while looking to the future. The Simonetta Ravizza woman is very confident and international. Growing up in Italy, I was very aware of the importance of *fare una bella figura* and this is an essential component of life. I think it is always important to present oneself well and then you are really free to let your personality shine.

For Simonetta Ravizza, "Don't follow the rules! Style is a question of personality," has always been my motto. This inspires me for future creations and collections.'

The Simonetta Ravizza showroom is in the heart of the Milan fashion world – Via Monte Napoleone – which the Italian designer calls a unique privilege and opportunity. In our interview, Simonetta reveals how it all began: 'My father Giuliano Ravizza started the fur company Annabella in 1957. As a child, I grew up fascinated by our family business and the world of high-end fashion. I witnessed how hard my father worked to build his business, and that has always been an inspiration to me. I started as a salesgirl among the other salesgirls at Annabella. It was such a wonderful learning experience and opportunity. I knew that I had a passion for fashion design and I wanted to explore it.

I began the Simonetta Ravizza line with the intention of building on my family tradition for high fashion while being creatively *avant-garde* and realising my artistic vision.

I am a wife and mother, who, like many modern women, tries to balance family life and work. Life in the fashion world is constantly busy!

I am very proud of my Italian roots and heritage, and I am inspired to provide the best of Italian culture and craftsmanship to the world. I am also fortunate that my work as a designer has taken me abroad. It has given me so many special opportunities to immerse myself in other cultures. I have been inspired by my travels to Russia, China, and glamorous ski locations. Designers always have to stay one step ahead of current life and, at Simonetta Ravizza, we have many new exciting ideas in mind for the future.'

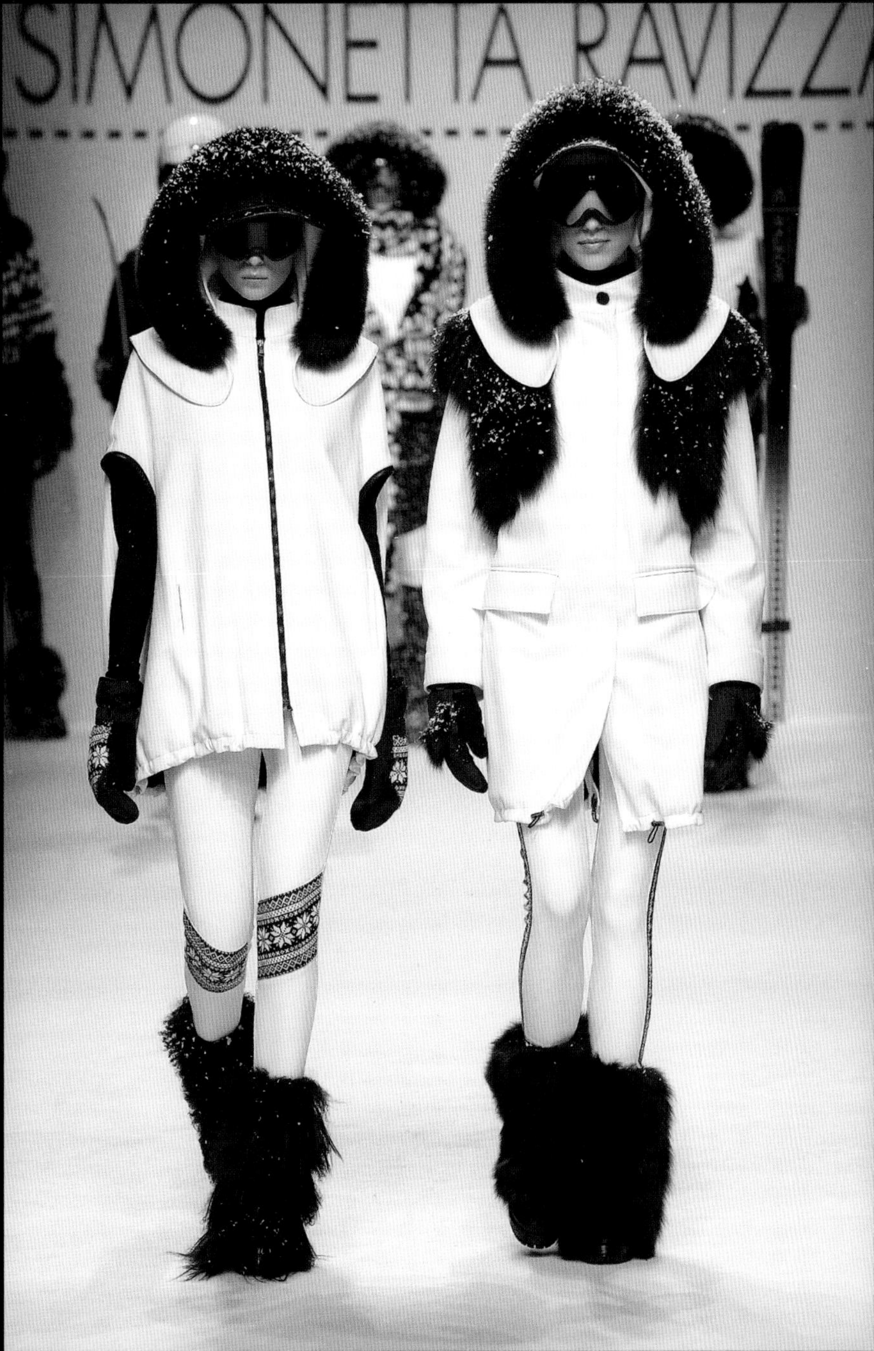
SIMONETTA RAVIZZA

SURF

**Do you want to control the waves?** Surfing is being a part of the ocean and being in harmony with nature. A surfer becomes a master of the water and rides the waves. A surfer tries to avoid falling or being overcome by the waves. Having muscular legs and strong arms helps a surfer control the water. There's a well-known principle every surfer learns: 'Nothing is softer or more flexible than water, yet nothing can resist it.'

Professional kitesurfer Rodolphe Mackeene tells us that surfing is more than just a sport and that it is more of a lifestyle or a philosophy. 'Imagine that you are only riding the waves

© Bogner

# Nothing is softer or more flexible than water, yet nothing can resist it.

for no longer than ten minutes, but that that ride takes hours of preparation. The time of actual surfing is short (maximum two or three hours), but the preparation is long and involves searching for the perfect location, choosing a comfortable outfit and mastering technical skills that allow you to sit on the board. A surfer can train his or her body by practising other sports such as pilates, spinning, kick boxing or karate. Having strong muscles is essential for a surfer on his/her surfboard.'

A surfer is exposed to strong sun and needs tanning products. In August 2013, *Vogue* New Zealand focused on the world of surfing and had an advertorial with the title 'Surf Goddess' in which they described the surf girl as posh, with flashy make up and in control over her body. The perfect surf babe is the ultimate dream for the surfer. The surf club is seen as the ideal place to meet your future girl or boy-friend.

Rodolphe Mackeene says that the image of the stereotypical blonde Californian surfer is no longer accurate and that everyone now can surf in nations ranging from the Caribbean, Indonesia, and Africa to Australia. Rodolphe says: 'The contemporary surfer now is also often a citizen of the big cities such as NY, Paris and London. Surfers today are hipsters, looking for a positive lifestyle. The idea of traditional surfing has also changed throughout the years: we have variants on surfing ranging from kitesurfing to snowboarding. The big brands in surf apparel face increased competition from emerging small brands like Mackeene, which offer elegant and practical clothes.'

© Michael Gramm

Experienced surfer Chris Verghote tells me why he loves the waves so much: 'There is the physical part that is exciting: surfing activates my whole body. I love the sport of surfing, but also cannot overlook the social aspect of surfing. Surfing is an activity I do with my best friends. I love the atmosphere in the water and on the beach.'

The sun and the waves are part of the world of surfing. So is the beach. Beach culture includes the perfect bathing suit or bikini for women and shorts for men.

Rodolphe Mackeene reveals why he started his own brand in swimwear: 'I was looking for the perfect outfit that would give me comfort and elegance. I wanted to create my own shorts to meet my demands. I understand that surfing is all about passion and spreads an inspiring philosophy to the sports lover. Current iconic names in surfing are Rob Machado, whose philosophy on surfing is great, and the athlete Kelly Slater, whose physical exploits are so admirable. Surfing has become the vision of an active and modern lifestyle shared by sportsmen and sportswomen all over the world. A surfer connects.'

© O'Neill

**Today, O'Neill is widely regarded as one of the world's leading active lifestyle brands.** While many things have changed since the company was founded by Jack O'Neill in 1952, one constant fact has remained: the brand's unshakable determination to inspire people and empower them with their passions. O'Neill builds technical gear and apparel for some of the world's top athletes and their followers. They are an American brand that wants to be relevant in the world of snowboarding and surfing. O'Neill's vision is to be the most authentic, progressive and distinctive brand in the sporting industry. Over sixty years ago, Jack O'Neill invented the wetsuit and gave birth to an industry out of a San Francisco garage on The Great Highway.

Tired of his routine job and because he wanted to spend more time in the water as a surfer, he opened the first surf shop in the garage. 'I just wanted to surf longer'.

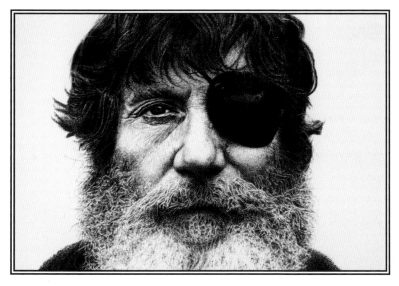

© O'Neill

Jack O'Neill is a true pioneer in the world of surf apparel. In Drew Kampion's book *It's Always Summer on the Inside*[**], O'Neill talks about his discovery of surfing: 'I was working downtown, and I just hated it. I'd get all screwed up, and then I'd come out to the west shore, and I'd jump in the ocean, and everything would be all right. I'd get one wave and I could go to sleep. I'd see that wall of water in my mind, and it just … put me to sleep.'

Jack's love of surfing started a long time ago when he first experienced a free ride on a wave along this stretch of beach between Venice and Santa Monica in the mid-1930s. He launched himself into a surge of white water and found himself racing shoreward. He was bodysurfing! Jack's life changed direction right then and there. He proclaims, 'I was being propelled by nature and it stuck with me.'

The invention of the wetsuit is no coincidence. Jack O'Neill found the answer to the question on the lips of every surfer. 'The water was so cold … and no rubber suit.' Jack O'Neill kept on believing in his invention and said: 'In the beginning, I had to give away wetsuits to get people to wear them.' This strategy helped and he became truly successful in selling wetsuits: 'There was a lot of interest in the wetsuits from all around the world. The O'Neill wetsuit and surfboard caused a real revolution in surfing. O'Neill Wetsuits Inc. sold the rights to the trademark to Logo International Inc. in 2007 and nowadays O'Neill is still market leader in wetsuits.' The slogan of O'Neill is, 'We make the world ride more because Jack did.' Keywords in the O'Neill brand are authenticity, spirit, joy, dedication and progression. O'Neill inspires sportsmen all over the world because Jack O'Neill and his family were pioneers in surfing. Their mission was and is to enable the world to ride more. The O'Neill products come

For Greater Warmth, Comfort and Bouyancy

COPIED YES …
DUPLICATED NEVER

** Jack O'Neill *It's Always Summer on the Inside* by Drew Kampion
© O'Neill

from the pursuit of innovative technology and a passion for riding. The O'Neill brand has many products: from wetsuits, surfboards, board bags, swimsuits, and clothing to shoes. Their philosophy is to bring their lifestyle to the sportsman. This lifestyle appeals to the trend-conscious surfer and snowboarder who wants to know all about the world of art, music and media. O'Neill surrounds itself with various artists from bands, singers and musicians to photographers and cameramen.

The O'Neill audience is young and has an active streak in mind and body. It's a mix of core and casual. O'Neill is also dedicated to creating a better, cleaner world and has therefore set up the O'Neill Sea Odyssey (1996) a free, ocean-based programme to educate young people about the marine environment. Jack O'Neill brings us back to the start of his passion for surfing: 'The three most important things in life: surf, surf, surf. First in, last out. When we started with the wetsuits, they laughed at us, but then they saw that the first person in with a wetsuit was the last person out of the water.'

# ═ Philipp Plein ═

Germans are conquering the world of sportswear with their strong reputation for high quality and originality. German fashion designer Philipp Plein was born in 1978; a self-confessed lover of football, he runs his fashion business in Lugano and his work is another example of the quality label MADE IN SWITZERLAND/ITALY/GERMANY. Plein started off designing steel and croc-print leather furniture and homeware in a rainbow of colours. A decade after the launch of his first fashion collection, Philipp Plein has evolved into a solid success story thanks to a fresh and cutting-edge aesthetic that swiftly cemented the brand's reputation. Philipp Plein's brand is unique, passionate and exclusive. The driving force of the company is human inspiration and creativity with the aim of setting trends rather than following them. This strong belief paved the way to becoming today's international lifestyle brand. 'Philipp Plein is a tribute to fashionable individualists who yearn to make their inner desires become reality,' says Plein. 'Life is too short to be insignificant!'. The young German designer is a self-described 'believer and dreamer.' Plein says that he pours his heart and soul into every aspect of the company. Championing the mantra 'luxury has to be fun'.

Philipp Plein took the world of fashion by storm and reveals how he entered this world. 'I entered the world of Fashion by mistake. It's a really long story but to cut

© Shutterstock

it short… I was a furniture designer and I used fashion to enrich my designs. The fashion pieces exhibited with my furniture became a huge success, which pushed me further in that direction.'

To build up a brand like this is a true success story. 'I created this brand out of nothing, without external help, this is why I am very proud of each development and of its success. I personally overview everything, from the designs to the visual merchandising in my stores and I couldn't imagine a different approach to work. I work 24 hours a day 365 days a year!'

The brand makes a striking reference to death with a skull as its emblem and double letters PP as its logo. 'I really like it! My initials framed by a hexagon are essential yet impactful. A typical collection for me is the quality of the fabrics and finishing, but most of all their personality.'

His clientele is varied. 'I don't have a particular goal except to continue to satisfy my customers all over the globe.' And the sudden success of his brand? 'Philipp Plein is a lifestyle brand made for people who love quality and luxury, but it's not only a fashion brand… it's a world. I like to entertain and to create escapes from reality, to stimulate people's imagination through spectacular fashion shows and fun events. For this reason, I always work with the best production agencies and creatives.'

He jokes about the fact that he is known as the darling of big football stars: 'I'm glad of it, athletes and fashion have always been connected and I'm proud when they choose to wear Philipp Plein as I'm a big football fan. That's why I'm also the official sponsor of A.C. Roma and Cagliari Calcio.'

Philipp Plein points out that he draws inspiration from the world of sports, but that he is more known for making casual clothes: 'My clothes are more casual than sporty, but I also have a line of tailor-made suits. Being a lifestyle brand, the range is wide.'

Philipp Plein reveals much about his enterprising personality in a metaphor about the sea: 'When you go diving, you see a lot of beautiful things – you have the reefs with the fish and the colourful corals. When you go deeper into the sea, it gets darker and it becomes dangerous, mysterious and exciting.'

# SWIMMING

**'I follow you, deep sea, baby', sings Lykki Li.** This song shows how passionate we are about water. Water is the natural environment for the swimmer who moves in the water against the flow or power of the water. A swimmer needs muscles and a powerful body to master the water and swim short or long distances. There are many possible movements ranging from butterfly and front crawl to backstroke and breaststroke. Hydrodynamics are an important factor in stroke technique and will make you swim faster. In order to be more hydrodynamic, people can increase the power of the strokes and water resistance. We all know that approximately 71% of Planet Earth is covered in water and further rising sea levels are expected due to global warming. Nature demands that we learn to live as amphibians on land and in water. So learning to swim is essential. Swimming gives us confidence to survive during natural disasters. On such occasions, a swimmer swims to survive. On a sporting level, look at swimming as the only exercise that keeps you fit without sweating. Only in swimming, you burn your fat without sweating. Swimming works out your whole body, improves cardiovascular conditioning and improves your body's use of oxygen without overworking the heart.

Swimming can also be a means of recreation that relieves tension. Floating relieves strain and relaxes your mind. A swimmer also experiences the joy of floating. By nature, we have the aptitude to be swimmers. Our body is naturally buoyant and requires little effort to float and swim. Even a new-born baby in water starts floating and is capable of swimming. Our future living environment is predicted to be spent under or on water. Swimming can be a social activity. Being able to swim means you can go for a swim, sunbathe, relax and socialise

© Mackeene

with people on beaches or in the best swimming pools around the world. It should not be a surprise that swimming adds to our physical and psychological well-being. In ancient times, bathing in hot water was seen as a means of preventing medical problems and increasing our mobility. Swimming also reduces pain and has been long known as a natural pain-killer for muscles and joint aches. Endurance, power, agility, balance and coordination are part of our swimming experience. If you want to know how to become a professional swimmer, it is a good idea to read the biographies of swimming stars Michael Phelps and Ian Thorpe because they are icons of contemporary swimming. Luckily, there is also a female super-star: American swimmer Missy Franklin. Becoming a star in swimming depends on many parameters. Training regularly and swimming at an early age, having an athletic body and being passionate about water sports: all help in becoming a strong swimmer. How to swim fashionably is not on every swimmer's lips.

The choice to swim elegantly or not depends on the person's sense of style. Halle Berry flirting with James Bond in *Die Another Day* with the perfect body in the perfect orange bikini says something about the relationship between swimwear and women. Fashion plays a part in synchronised swimming or artistic swimming where women execute graceful movements in the water.

Sunglasses and swimwear make us dream of movie stars and top models.

© Patrizia Pepe

**Speedo is a brand with a rich history** and proves that retired sea captain Jim Parson chose the right name for the company in 1928 when he suggested the name 'Speed on in your Speedos.' From manufacturer of socks for the Australian Army during World War I to producer of swimwear, Speedo is undoubtedly the leader in swimwear. Technological innovations that helped swimmers worldwide to perform at peak level and win a record number of Olympic titles in swimming made the company an international success. Speedo is now a multinational that has grown fast since its founder Alexander MacRae, a young Scot, set up the first factory in 1914 in Regent Street, Sydney. At this time MacRae named his brand 'Fortitude', taken from his family crest. In 1928 the company shifted from the production of socks to a range of swimwear. The first technological innovation was introduced in the 1920s when MacRae introduced the classic, figure-hugging 'Racerback' costume, the world's first non-wool suit.

The 'Racerback' allows greater freedom of movement, allowing wearers to swim faster. Swedish swimmer Arne Borg set a world record in Speedo swimwear, establishing the brand in the hearts and minds of swimmers and the general public. More Olympic wins and world records for Australia would follow in the 1930s. During World War Two, over 90% of Speedo's manufacturing output was devoted to the war effort. The goods made included knitwear, underwear, mosquito nets and signal flags. An increasing number of athletes in the 1950s chose to endorse the Speedo brand and transformed Speedo into a world famous brand with the start of exports to the USA in 1959. The brand continued to grow during the 1960s with more countries competing in Speedo swimwear. The 1970s brought the introduction of nylon and elastane, which is still the most popular swimwear fabric today.

During the 1980s an historic agreement was signed between China and Speedo, providing training wear and equipment for the Chinese athletic team and later Speedo was retitled as a global sports lifestyle brand – Speedo International Ltd.

1996 saw the launch of the Speedo AQUABLADE, featuring 8% lower surface resistance than S2000. Speedo also launched the revolutionary FASTSKIN swimsuit inspired by shark skin. Its award-winning design was worn by many of the world's top swimmers including Grant Hackett, Michael Klim, Inge de Bruijn, Lenny Krayzelburg and Michael Phelps. At the 2000 Sydney Olympics 13 of the 15 World Records and 83% of all swimming medals were won by swimmers competing in Speedo FASTSKIN swimsuits.

A limited edition anniversary collection was modelled on high profile names including models Jerry Hall, Naomi Campbell and Yasmin Le Bon. In 2004, Speedo launched FASTSKIN FSII swimsuit – an evolution of FASTSKIN. Michael Phelps made history at the 2004 Athens Olympics by becoming the first ever swimmer to win 8 medals at the Olympics (six gold, two bronze) wearing FASTSKIN FSII. More swimmers in Athens wore Speedo than all other brands combined. The legacy continued with the launch of Fastskin FS-PRO in 2007 – the fastest and most powerful lightweight suit on the market and 21 world records were broken within 6 months.

In 2008, Speedo launched LZR RACER®. The suit changed the face of swimming, and was famously worn by Michael Phelps as he won 8 Gold medals at the Beijing Olympics.

Michael Phelps won his 23rd gold medal at the 2016 Rio Olympic Games, becoming the most decorated Olympian of all time. In 2018 Speedo celebrates its 90th Anniversary. Speedo makes us dream of the perfect swimsuit and the power brand hopes to continue to develop the technology and fashion of swimwear.

© Shutterstock

© Mackeene

# Harold Mackeene

'Beachwear is all about innovation!' says Harold Mackeene, who wants to find his place among the giants of sportswear thanks to his innovations in beachwear. As a new player, Mackeene stepped into the beachwear game in 2006 together with his brother Rodolphe who is a professional kitesurfer. The Scottish-French Mackeene brothers weren't able to find swim shorts that 'combined elegance, style, comfort and speedy drying' on their travels and found the solution by creating them themselves. The first line from Mackeene sees to all the little details (seams, stitching, braids, magnetic zips, rivets, anodised metallic buttons) and is made from an exclusive elastic high quality material available in 22 colours.

With great ideas about what the perfect short for men could look like and with no more than a few hundred euros, they were able to start their own company, which drew the support of an investor. www.Mackeene.com is an internet site for online sales of their collections of beach and swimwear. The traditional buyer may find the Mackeene bathing suit, shorts, polos and accessories in shops from Miami to Paris; prices start at €135.

The designers say that they create shorts 'like a second skin' with a straight cut and use of innovative materials such as stretch, magnets replacing zips and drying nanotechnology in combination with environmentally-friendly fabrics. The brand is the first in the textile industry to use nanotechnology to prevent the fibre from absorbing water. The fabric becomes hydrophobic. Harold Mackeene loves nature and wants to keep the natural environment clean for the swimmer or surfer by reducing damage to the environment.

© Mackeene

© Mackeene

This green policy is reflected in Mackeene's choice of colours and fabrics.

In 2012 Mackeene had devised a collection called 'BEE' in remembrance of the bees that had been killed by pesticides. Thus he hopes to help maintain a green space or *un espace vert*. As an entrepreneur, Mackeene dreams of a complete environmentally-friendly collection that combines nanotechnology with natural materials such as linen or banana. Nanotechnology coating does not affect the fibre.

Harold Mackeene is the first designer in sportswear who uses nanotechnology to keep your swimsuit or shorts dry: 'We did the test in his Parisian office near the Louvre and spilled water on a Kleenex tissue and on paper with nanotechnology. The result was phenomenal: the water is immediately absorbed by the normal fibre whereas the fabric with nanotechnology is water-repellent. Staying dry on the beach is part of the Mackeene vision. This technology was a Belgian invention that was used in the American army. Thanks to Mackeene it will add to your comfort in and around the water. Every detail is the result of a long creative process. From the magnets replacing the traditional zip to the fabrics. Mackeene targets the sports lover aged 30-40 who wants comfort and luxury.'

Harold jokes: 'Most men like beachwear that makes them not look like an adolescent, but like an adult looking for style and quality. Our clients are opinion-leaders who want the best and who are looking for products instead of brands. We have the sportive guy in mind who takes care of his body. There is something for everyone. We have three lengths in our shorts. There is the long typically American short, the classic in middle-length and the short trendy version. My icon at the beach is the American actor Steve McQueen in the 1970s. I try to conjure up his elegance and sex appeal.'

Mackeene opens up a world of water, sun and comfort. Passionate about design and fashion, Harold MacKeene bases his style on the Mackeene collections known as Mackeene. His training in France and experience in China as a graphic designer help him to design. His brother Rodolphe, an accomplished kitesurfer, brings 'technical expertise'. Nothing has been left to chance in their effort to attract men to the brand. Harold smiles: 'We are exclusive, but not too exclusive. We create for the person who wants to be chic while doing sports. We are there for this clientele.

Gone are the days when swimsuits were impractical and looked old-fashioned. Surfers across the world were waiting for innovation and style. We bring new ideas to beachwear. We started in St. Barts, produce our swimwear in Portugal and are ready to conquer the world. We are becoming a solid brand thanks to our strategy to be environmentally-friendly, elegant and new.'

© Mackeene

# GOLF

**Golf is a stylish sport.** Golf is an attractive pursuit for men and women alike. P.G. Wodehouse once said, 'Golf is happiness.' This is also the name for his collection of short stories describing his golf experiences. P.G. Wodehouse considers a love of golf essential in the relationship between a man and a woman. He sees golf as a metaphor for life: the competition between two men in plus fours determines the future of their beloveds.

Golfer and golf apparel designer Ruben Opheide tells us about his own passion for golf: 'Golf is an inspiring sport. Many people around the world call golf "the greatest game ever played".

© Shutterstock

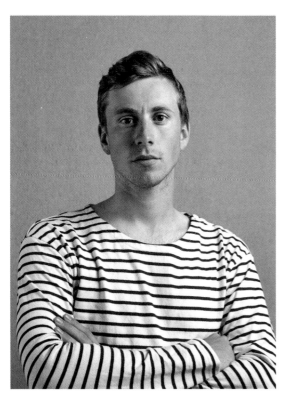
© Ruben Opheide

Simply because for so many people, golf is much more than a sport or hobby. It is a lifestyle. It's hard to express why this game is so addictive to most people. I believe it is the unique combination of technical difficulty, stunning outdoor settings and the general good life. Golf is therapy. After a stressful week in the office, golf truly is the only occupation that clears the head completely. Most people can play golf on a good level well into their '60s or '70s. Injuries are usually rare, compared to most other popular sports in Europe such as football and tennis.'

Ruben stresses the importance of social contacts while playing golf: 'Also, business will flourish when you play golf. Many people at your local club are businessmen or entrepreneurs. When you meet people at the golf club, they easily become friends.'

Sportswear brands have discovered that golf apparel is a lucrative business. Adidas, Nike, Hugo Boss and Puma have added a golf line to their businesses. Tiger Woods worked together with Nike and is known to wear his traditional red polo during the last round of a tournament, because his mother Kutida told him that this colour would give him extra energy. Golf apparel is very innovative: Scandinavian brands Galvin Green, Johan Lindeberg, Abacus and Kjus have paved the way for the use of new high-quality materials in addition to traditional cotton. Adidas recognises the importance of golf and has started up the subsidiary TaylorMade, to promote and sell golf apparel. Puma's answer to this strategy has been the launch of flashy, colourful and new designs for its Cobra collection. New trends in golf apparel were launched by the Belgian entrepreneur, Ruben Opheide, who reintroduced 'plus fours' or retro 'golf knickers'.

© Bogner

The collection of the finest golf clothes is inspired by the 1920s and 1930s. Socks, golf knickers, polos, sweaters and even matching headwear can be purchased in the online store. Owner Ruben Opheide says: 'Golf has a long tradition of specialised attire that was being worn by Scottish aristocrats who loved to swing their golf clubs and take in the fresh air of the incredible Scottish nature. We are proud to share our passion for golf and fashion. I bring a real discovery for the golf lover who wants to combine his love of new trends with respect for the traditional world of golf. Golf attire is being influenced by trends of function and durability. Golfers are showing a preference for moisture-wicking fabrics, crisp details, and trendy design. Golf is a sport with a tremendous history. Professional golfers usually have a combination of talent, dedication and great team care. Professional golfers are usually so good compared to the average amateur, it's frustrating and promising at the same time.'

# BOSS
## HUGO BOSS

**HUGO BOSS and sport look like the ideal marriage.** Let us take a look at HUGO BOSS' love of sports. We find not only the high-profile sports campaigns (for example with top football players Mario Gomez and Serdar Tasci as Hugo Boss models) but, more importantly, the Company has had the BOSS Green line since 2004. BOSS Green was originally designed with golf in mind, but since then BOSS Green has gone on to draw inspiration from many other sporting activities and has expanded its clientèle to everyone who loves its *sportive* character. It is a fact that BOSS Green sports the active look. BOSS Green represents golf-inspired sportswear for men and women that pairs classic cuts with refreshing designs in bold colours. The line successfully bridges the gap between fashionable sports apparel and sportswear fashion.

HUGO BOSS is one of the global leaders in the apparel market for premium men's and womenswear and is known worldwide for distinctive, innovative fashion statements. With a presence in over 127 countries and with its brands BOSS, HUGO, BOSS Orange and BOSS Green, the company stands for outstanding design and a high-quality product. The BOSS core brand has been the driving force behind the company's success for many years. Hugo Ferdinand Boss first started his clothing company in 1924 in Metzingen, where it is still based, a small town south of Stuttgart, Germany. After his death in 1948, the business progressively expanded under the guidance of his son-in-law Eugen Holy, and in the 1950s the business turned its hand to making men's suits. The timing was perfect – the male fashion industry was just establishing itself and throughout the 1960s and 1970s, BOSS suits became the benchmark for quality, fashionable menswear. In 2007, international private equity firm Permia acquired the company from the Valentino Fashion Group. BOSS Green has become a popular line, with BOSS Green items specifically designed for a sporty look.

BOSS Green has an extensive collection of outerwear, knitwear, sweaters, jerseys, trousers, shoes and accessories. With BOSS Green it is easy to find the right garment for your activity, whether it is sport or leisure. BOSS Green's watchwords are lifestyle, quality and performance.

The HUGO BOSS brands are generally known around the world as the epitome of style. HUGO BOSS' passion for and knowledge of designer clothes really shines through in all they do. Sign up to BOSS Green and you'll be a style guru overnight! You can order the label BOSS Green online. And it's nearly as quick as going out and picking up a BOSS Green product yourself. The great thing about the BOSS Green collection is its variety. There are BOSS Green sneakers, BOSS Green jackets, with and without hoods, and a whole range of BOSS Green jumpers in different colours and with v-necks or crew necks, zipped and unzipped. And, as for BOSS Green polo neck shirts, there's a whole range of colours and designs on offer.

# The great thing about the Boss Green collection is its variety

© Steven Deduytsche

# Steven Deduytsche

Steven Deduytsche is a fairly new player in the range of golf accessories. Being an experienced golf player, he discovered the need for an elegant and attractive range of golf bags and developed them himself. Looking for the balance between the aesthetics of fashion and the technical perfection of sportswear in golf accessories, he launched his line of Steven Deduytsche golf bags. Steven says: 'I did this because golf was my passion and because there was no perfect golf equipment around.' His slogans are 'golf meets fashion' and 'make an impression on the golf course.' His bags come in two colours: black and white, and are made of leather. His bags can be personalised and bear the name of the owner. He says: 'The SDD bags fulfilled the need for elegance and style in golf attire. Black and white are beautiful and posh colours and have always been present in my logo. After improving my own skills in golf, I became more passionate about the sport and so I discovered the world of golf accessories.'

Steven Deduytsche has played golf since 2007 and has been golf-minded for much longer. Why is Steven so passionate about golf? 'Theoretically, anyone can win a game. I could beat Tiger Woods. Even a handicapped person could. That makes golf so exciting!' He compares golf to life and says that nothing is easy in life. 'It takes time and passion to score. You have to hit a few into the woods to appreciate the game,

© Steven Deduytsche

© Steven Deduytsche

much like life'. No surprise then that he participates in the Mercedes Golf Trophy. He now consolidates his position on the market of luxury brands and golf accessories. The first 4 years in the business of luxury brands were meant to position his brand. Steven Deduytsche has reached his break-even already in only three years. A success story! How did Steven Deduytsche manage to do this? He smiles and says that he uses the image of himself on the speedboat in the Blue Sea. As a speedboat racer, he started off in the Red Ocean full of competitors. He moved on from there to the Blue Ocean and now experiences better times.

As a captain of a speedboat you have to steer your boat. Especially in times of a major crisis, you need to reposition your brand and look at what the competition is doing. He has launched his own brand of luxury bags and range of golf accessories with the slogan: 'First things, first'.

A brand needs a name, a logo, a story behind it and a good business plan every year. Starting a brand requires finances. You can only convince investors with a good business plan. He leads his company with five senses that helped him to build an iconic brand. According to Steven Deduytsche, marketing involves the five senses: sight, touch,

hearing, taste and smell. 'My products are of good quality and activate the five senses.'

As CEO of his own brand, he oversees every aspect of the production: from design to sales. He is in full control. In the fashion world, he has gained his leading position in Belgium because he oversees every activity by his staff, from designers to the salespeople in the flagship store. He oversees the work of his designers and is in full control of his products: the SDD bags and golf accessories. Steven does not believe in giving full liberty to his designers. 'I am so concerned with good image that I don't allow the designers to ruin this. Steven Deduytsche controls and checks everything. Every golf bag is leather and has a waterproof zip. Luxury-seekers will find what they are looking for.'

Steven's fascination with leather began as as student at the renowned Vlerick Business School when he discovered the superiority of the material. The craftsmanship and durability that are needed when you produce leather goods inspired him to enter the business in 2009. The worlds of both fashion and accessories use leather, which is a natural product that requires intensive work. Steven Deduytsche clearly relies on a long tradition of superior leather goods made in Belgium.

# CYCLING

**Cycling has many associations, both good and bad.** From the excellent performances by true champions to the doping scandals that shook the Tour de France. Cycling is very accessible to many, since recreational cyclists require only a bike to ride on. Every child wants to learn to ride his or her bike and it is a real family occasion when the child learns to ride. A round of applause for the biker! It may be the start of a true career in cycling. Eddy Merckx is probably the greatest champion, winning the Tour de France five times. Scandal-struck Lance Armstrong did not manage to beat him. Can the Briton Froome beat Merckx in winning the most titles? Cycling is so widespread and popular in Europe that they even made an animated movie about it. The film 'The Triplets of Belleville' tells the story of Madame Souza, an elderly woman who goes on a quest to rescue her champion grandson, a Tour de France cyclist, who has been kidnapped by the French mafia for gambling purposes and taken to the city of Belleville. The film was nominated for two Academy Awards – Best Animated Feature and Best Original Song for 'Belleville Rendez-vous.' Spanish racer Alberto Contador called Paris Roubaix the most beautiful race to watch. Other important one-day races include the Amstel Gold Race, Milan-San Remo, and the Tour of Flanders. Of course there is also the legendary Tour de France, covering 3 exciting weeks.

Winning major European competitions is often the result of resilience, says Belgian cyclist Tom Boonen in the magazine *Procycling 2013*. 'What matters in cycling is that you believe in yourself. Its's all about running away from your competitor and winning! Defeat or injuries should not stop your belief in yourself.' The Tour of Flanders and Roubaix made him legendary as hero of the cobblestones.

Wearing the perfect outfit helps make you a winner. Let us go back to the early days of cycling (1890s) when women wearing bloomers and riding bicycles were regarded as outrageous.

Women in pants defied the difference in clothing for men and women. Riding style for women was side-saddle, covering the legs and ankles with a skirt. The big change for women and cycling came in the 1920s when women started to wear trousers for cycling as well as for skiing or hiking. Cycling has now come so far from its start and is now all about fashion statements. Starting with the Spandex shorts worn in the Tour de France to the spandex shorts under André Agassi's tennis outfit. Spandex has definitely become more than just a fabric: it is now a trendsetter that promises comfort and of course victory in competition!

If you want to cycle, embrace the sport in the wonderful races you can follow on TV or as a supporter at the roadside.

A popular variation of cycling is spinning. Spinning can be an addictive form of exercise. As a female spinner I want to explain why: 'I feel the adrenaline from spinning. I became addicted to cycling to music with a teacher in front of me who gave instructions. I like to turn up the resistance level because the tougher the ride, the more calories I lose. Spinning to music is my way of getting rid of the pressure and stress in my life. I lost so much weight that I love my new body and am in shape again. Spinning is always on my to-do list. Spinning is like ecstasy!' Famous celebrity spinning enthusiasts include Lady Gaga, Katie Holmes, Charlize Theron and Jake Gyllenhaal. The websites of some famous spinning studios are www.flywheel.com and www.soulcycle.com

## The Assos slogan 'Sponsor Yourself' speaks for itself. Assos' philosophy states that, 'The primary objective is not for the garment to last forever, but first and foremost to maximise total comfort when in the saddle. Your time, your ride, is what really counts. Enabling you to ride in total comfort and well-protected is what makes the Assos difference. Consequently, we use performance-oriented fabrics to construct highly technical garments that are light, low volume and sensitive. Not rigid, bulletproof stuff! Assos' apparel is precious: functional, high-tech and, yes, it may be more delicate than ordinary cycling gear. All this to increase your well-being and pleasure when cycling, be it for fitness or for racing purposes.'

Assos is a Swiss brand that launched its first aero one-piece skin suit in 1976, followed by the first lycra cycling shorts and first bib shorts pattern design in the same year. In 1988 Assos created its first multi-density insert, T. Campionissimo. Later inventions were the first stabiliser rear mesh insert in 1995, the first elastic cycling short insert that created the S-2 comfort revolution in 1998. The first choose-your-comfort application concept in 2002 was followed by the NEXT Assos cycling shorts in 2007. In 2014, Assos launched the Experience Royal Comfort or Game Changer S. 'In terms of total comfort, using the proper cycling shorts is more important than the bike you're riding. Don't compromise!' Assos Equipment is engineered to handle high mileage in different climate conditions. The garment you have purchased is made for true cycling, made to last many kilometres, but there is a price to pay! That price is a little bit of loving care and understanding. Because of its high performance DNA, Assos is not made to last forever, but by observing the following simple but essential guidelines, you can extend your garment's lifespan and take full advantage of what Assos is capable of doing for your well-being.

© Assos

Assos gives its riders advice in memorable one-liners and invites cyclists to 'Move into the riding position and feel the garment "click" onto your body.' Cut anatomically without movement restrictions when on the bike, Assos garments are designed to fit a cyclist's body. If you don't have an athletic body, Assos will not fit you the same way. Its pattern design is anatomically shaped according to the Assos AEPD philosophy. AEPD stands for Advanced, Ergonomic, Pattern, Design. Assos contours your body, protecting it without applying pressure when you are on your bicycle. Assos' technical garments are not intended for leisure, but for cycling. It is important to pick the right size – when a garment is too small, seams and fabric are put under too much stress, which will result in fabric deterioration and pilling. If you have never worn Assos before, I highly recommend visiting an Assos point of sale in order to determine your proper size before purchasing. Don't forget to put on Assos Chamois crème as pre-ride protection or Skin repair gel after your tour on your bike. Have a good ride!

© Daniel Levitte

# = Rick Owens =

Rick Owens became known as the wonder-child of American fashion with his 'brutal chic', a style using exaggerations and contrasts. Owens launched his own label in 1994 and has gained respect in the fashion world from NY to Paris and London.

Sportswear has been a constant source of inspiration for the Californian, but his relationship to sports and sportswear did not start easily. 'I grew up an ultra-sensitive, effeminate, only child in a small provincial town in central California. When choosing sides for team sports in school, I was considered so undesirable I was simply not chosen at all and allowed to sit and read. So sports took on the allure of an inaccesible masculine world for me.'

© Owens corp

So how did he change his attitude towards sports? 'As an adult, I joined the gym, changed my body and learned how to be comfortable in an all-male environment. As a designer, I took conventional sportswear and exaggerated it – pumping basketball sneakers up like monster trucks and over-sizing shorts and T-shirts to Kabuki-like proportions. I suppose all this was originally about fitting in, but later it was about fitting in on my own terms, and maybe fitting in with a bit of irony.'

Does Rick Owens know the secret behind the love affair between men and sportswear? 'All men want to appear dynamic. A sports-wear look allows a man a hint of virility that is maybe earned or maybe not. I like sports in general as a healthier expression of a man's undeniably competitive nature than war.'

© Owens corp

© Owens corp

# POLO

**All you need to play polo** is a ball, a stick, a horse and four players who know the rules of the game. Polo is an equestrian game with four riders and their mounts that originates in Iran, where nobility of the Rang Dynasty played in the 5th Century BC. Polo was a training game for cavalry units that were usually the King's guards or elite troops. Polo has been an elite sport from its very beginnings and it is no surprise that the most famous polo players nowadays are the English royals Prince Charles and his sons, Prince William and Prince Harry.

Alexander the Great, who conquered the Persian Empire around the year 331BC, was a keen player. When his rival, Darius of Persia, suggested he should stay at home and play polo, Alexander replied: 'I am the stick – the ball is the world.' Darius soon regretted his taunts. The first recorded game took place between the Turkomans and the Persians. The game was won by the Turkomans. Polo spread in the 7th Century from its home in Iran to China and Japan. By the 16th Century, the Persian Emperor Babur established the game in India. In 1868, British tea planters discovered the game in Manipur on the Burmese border with India. From India it spread to England. The first polo club in the world was formed by British tea planters at Silchar, west of Manipur. The oldest existing polo club was also founded in India and was the Calcutta Polo Club Aldershot. There has recently been a popular renaissance of the game in India, with many of the old princely states and families taking up the sport of their fathers. The first polo club in England was Monmouthshire, founded in 1872 by Capt. Francis "Tip" Herbert (1845 – 1922), 7th Lancers, at his brother's seat, Clytha Park, near Abergavenny. Today, polo is played in 80 countries worldwide. It was an Olympic sport from 1900 to 1939 and has now been recognised again by the International Olympic Committee. Polo is, however, played professionally in Argentina, Australia, Brazil, Canada, Chile, Dominican Republic, France, Germany, Iran, India, New Zealand, Mexico, Pakistan, Jamaica, Spain, Switzerland, the United Kingdom and the U.S. Polo is unique among team sports, in that amateur players often play alongside the sport's top professionals. Men and women can also play on the same game. The most important tournaments – at club level – are La Triple Corona in Argentina and in England, the Hurlingham Cup. In the States, you have the United States Polo Association, which is the country's governing body for polo. The first polo match in the U.S was at Dickell's Riding Academy at 39th Street and Fifth Avenue in NYC. The first Polo Club in the US was established in 1876 and it was here that the first American outdoor polo match took place. Polo in the States became a high-speed sport and differed from the game in the UK, where it involves short passes to move the ball forward toward the opponents' goal.

In Europe polo is now rapidly expanding. Almost every capital has its polo club. Polo has always been a game played by kings and princes. Dare to be like a king or prince yourself and try polo!

© Shutterstock

## POLO
### RALPH LAUREN

**Ralph Lauren was the official outfitter for Wimbledon in 2016** and seems to be the personification of the American dream. To *American Vogue* he explained where he finds inspiration: 'I have always been inspired by the dream of American families in the country, weathered trucks and farmhouses; sailing off the coast of Maine; following dirt roads in an old wood-panelled station wagon; a convertible filled with young college kids sporting crew cuts and sweatshirts and frayed sneakers.'

While most people are familiar with the name Ralph Lauren, he was born Ralph Lifshitz to Belarusian immigrants on October 14th, 1939 in the Bronx. His father was an artist who would occasionally paint houses. Ralph developed a sense of style early on. As such, he treasured his siblings' hand-me-downs and with his own money he bought clothes at the local army surplus store and worked at a department store. The idea of fashion design was new. 'The world isn't ready for Ralph Lauren', said the designer. Almost half a century later, we know that the world is ready for the American designer who became one of the most celebrated talents on the American fashion scene.

The polo pony is immortalised by Lauren because he considered polo an international, sophisticated sport. Lauren started off his career with a collection of ties that has grown into an entirely new clothing brand, redefining American style. Ralph Lauren has always stood for providing quality products, creating worlds and inviting people to take part in his brand's vision. Ralph Lauren was the innovator of lifestyle advertisements that tell a story and the first to create stores that encourage customers to participate in that lifestyle.

Looking back, Mr Lauren is satisfied with his career. 'Back when all this started, I felt sure that there were no boundaries. I'm even more sure of that today.' In 2000, Ralph Lauren designated his classic icon, the Polo Pony, as the symbol for the Pink Pony Campaign and sent his models down the runway wearing Pink Pony shirts.

What is the story behind Ralph Lauren's Pink Pony? Mr. Lauren opens up to me about the idea. "The Pink Pony is the symbol for our battle against cancer. The Royal Marsden partners with Ralph Lauren Corporation to develop a world-class breast cancer research facility. The Royal Marsden, the largest and most comprehensive cancer centre in Europe, and Ralph Lauren Corporation are proud partners in funding a state-of-the-art breast cancer research facility. The new centre will be dedicated to advancing breast cancer research with the goal of improving early diagnosis and the development of new treatments for breast cancer.

'Fighting breast cancer has been a long-standing goal of mine,' says Lauren. 'I am so pleased and honoured for our company to partner with The Royal Marsden, a truly remarkable institution with a global reputation for ground-breaking research and pioneering the very latest in cancer treatments and technologies. It is my great hope that this partnership advances cancer treatment options and outcomes for patients around the world.'

The Ralph Lauren Centre for Breast Cancer Research will take up a whole floor in the historic Royal Marsden Hospital, which will be developed to the highest specification to provide a world-class facility for breast cancer research. The Centre's overall goal will be to identify molecular differences between tumours that allow the optimal treatment of individual breast cancer patients and thereby reduce recurrence and mortality from the disease and eliminate unnecessary toxicity. This partnership continues a long-standing relationship between The Royal Marsden and Ralph Lauren Corporation: after all, The Royal Marsden benefited from the Ralph Lauren Corporation's Pink Pony for many years.

# ═ Hackett ═

Travelling to London, I talk to Mr Jeremy Hackett about his life, and his label Hackett. 'I grew up in Bristol and left school at seventeen with my father's words ringing in my ears: 'If you don't pull your socks up you will end up working in a shop'. Fortunately, although to my father's dismay, that is is exactly what happened. Whilst at school, I had a Saturday job in a local tailor's and my boss generously offered me a full-time job. I soon realised that if I wanted to make a success of my life in the clothing business I would need to move to London which I duly did aged nineteen. I worked in a number of boutiques along the then fashionable Kings Road before taking up a position in Savile Row where I really began to learn about tailoring, cloth and the rarified customers. I worked for John Michael, an inspirational retailer who was the first person to teach me about what a brand meant before the word became commonly bandied about. I had always been interested in vintage clothes and made regular forays to the London street markets picking up classic suits, tweed jackets, riding kit and formal dress, along with hand-made shoes and luggage. It was the seventies and the pickings were good, it was only a hobby but useful extra cash at the time. I then went into partnership with a friend of mine Ashley Lloyd-Jennings and we opened a shoe shop in Covent Garden and sold Alden, Sperry, Edward Green shoes and Belgian shoes. Unfortunately it was before Covent Garden had got going and after three tough years we shut up our shop. I then took a job waiting on tables, the toughest job I have ever had, but I learnt a lot about service, which still remains with me today. I began to start buying second-hand clothes again with Lloyd-Jennings and we sold them on to a friend in Paris. Before long it struck us that it would be more profitable to sell the clothes in London. We opened our first shop in Fulham, an up-and-coming district, but one our bank manager described as a retailers graveyard, with no business plan, no marketing plan and very little money. For six months we traded without a name over the door; because our last venture had been called Lloyd-Jennings, we finally decided to call it Hackett.'

Hackett is clearly influenced by the world of sports, so I wanted to know if Mr Hackett is a sportsman. 'It's an awfully long time since I have taken part in any sport, the most arduous exercise I take part in today is walking the dogs. At school I was a keen sportsman, I played rugby, tennis and cricket, I was a good runner and swimmer and I cycled a fair bit. I was also fairly adept at table football. In my twenties I learnt to ride, not so much for the riding but all the kit and tack that went with it; I was never very good. I took part in team chases, hunted a bit and was fortunate to have lessons from rider William Fox-Pitt, whom we sponsored at the time. I broke my leg out hunting one day and that was the end of my riding days. Today, though, I am a very good spectator.' Mr. Hackett continues to talk about about how sportswear influenced his work: 'It is difficult not to be influenced by sportswear as it has become such a major part of many men's wardrobes. Considering that most of our partnerships have a connection with sport, such as the Army Polo, London Rowing Club, Aston Martin Racing, Queen's Tennis and the Formula One team Williams Martini Racing, it is unavoidable, but it is the execution that is important.'

Mr Hackett shares his view on the link between high fashion, ready-to-wear and sportswear: 'It is inevitable that high fashion and sportswear would team up because it is a vast and lucrative market and as men continue to dress in a more relaxed manner, then the fusing of the two makes sense. Most of our business is conducted in tailoring but because the Hackett Polo shirt is so visually dominant, people assume we are a sportswear brand. I remember when we first sponsored Polo I thought, who is going to buy a shirt emblazoned with Hackett on it? How wrong I was – people bought them in droves. I would never have considered making the shirts unless we were involved in the sport. I wanted it to be authentic and to be credible, after all it is my name. I think that it is vitally important for the brand's integrity that whatever sportswear products we make are of the best fit and quality.

We have also created a range of clothing sportswear, entitled Aston Martin Racing by Hackett, with the attention to detail that you would expect for a brand such as Aston Martin. We have used high-spec technical fabrics and have taken sportswear to a luxury level. Working with Aston Martin has helped Hackett to raise our game and who wouldn't wish to work with the most famous British brand in the world... apart from Hackett of course.'

© Hackett

# SAILING

**Sailing and fishing are the best-known nautical sports** with a connection to fashion. Sailors have inspired fashion designers such as Coco Chanel and Jean Paul Gaultier who dared to wear the striped T-shirts worn by French sailors from Brittany! Sailing evokes passion for the sea and induces both relaxation and challenge. Sailing can be done by an amateur who enjoys the view of the sea offered by a weekend sailing trip or by a professional competing with other sailors. A professional sailor in Holland who participated in the Olympic Games for his country, tells us: 'I couldn't sail on my own and asked a friend. My love for sailing was big from the very start, and I found it relaxing and wonderful to sail. The best experience you get from sailing is to sail away from the harbour and sail on the motion of the wind when the engine is switched off.' Sailing partners are well adjusted to each other because it is important to know your sailing partner when you enter a competition together. The coastlines of Normandy and Southern England offer nice places to sail. The coastline of the Mediterranean, spanning Croatia, Turkey, France

© Shutterstock

and Italy, is impressive for sailors from around the world, too. A warm climate and nice natural surroundings add to the beauty of your sailing trip. Nothing is more beautiful than an isolated port in a deserted bay where you can spend the night. The best sailing trip is hard to describe but creates a special feeling.

However, sailing is not always without danger. Storms or accidents on board are possible risks. Sailing has been said to be 'the most expensive way to get somewhere you don't want to be'. This reflects the time needed to sail a certain distance when the wind and its direction do not always lead you where you want to go.

One of the most prestigious sailing competitions is undoubtedly the Americas Cup series, in which the Prada boat Luna Rossa took part. In an interview with the Boat Show in summer 2014, Prada CEO Patrizio Bertelli talks about Luna Rossa's participation. 'Sailing is an illness, and let's hope it's a healthy illness. It is important for us as a group to be part of it and also to be part of tradition. Prada represents Italy no matter what the budget issues are. Our goal is to sail to win. Our goal has always been lofty, and all we want to do is to represent quality.'

© Shutterstock

**Founded in 1976 by the Dini family, Paul & Shark is synonymous today** with Italian elegance and style, with its Men's, Women's, Children's and Accessories collections available in 73 different countries. From the very beginning, integrated production determined the quality of the label. On 4 March 1957 the 'Maglificio Daco' mill, founded in 1921, opened its doors once again under new owner Gian Ludovico Dini who, nine years later, changed its name to Dama S.p.A. Every aspect of production took place within the company, from producing yarns to making the boxes used to package the clothing. Items were even shipped all over the world thanks to a prestigious partnership with Christian Dior and Balenciaga.

At the start of the 1970s Paolo Dini, the eldest son of Gian Ludovico, happened to find himself in a small sailmaker's workshop during a trip to Maine, where the sail from an old 18th-century clipper caught his eye. Its inscription read Paul&Shark: it was fate.

The brand's aim has always been to seek excellence both in the quality of its products and the manufacture of its materials, guaranteeing a rigorous selection process based on exacting standards. Paul&Shark creates sportswear, smart casual and luxury lines, combining technical fabrics with elegant and stylish details. The yachting collection dates back to the mid-1970s, when Paul&Shark launched in the sports fashion sector with a collection inspired by the world of sailing and based on its elegance, performance and

© Willem De Meyer

spirit of adventure. In 1978, its CoP918 pullover was born: a sailing sweater that would go on to become an icon of the Paul&Shark style.

Instantly recognisable from its packaging, a metal can used on board ships as a multi-purpose container, this garment saw immediate success and signalled the start of a whole new water-repellent knitwear collection.

Over the years, the company has expanded greatly to become a comprehensive luxury sportswear range, appreciated by fans of Italian fashion and high-performance technical materials, many of which have been patented by Paul&Shark.

Today, Paul and Shark is a true international brand, with more than 280 Paul&Shark monobrand boutiques located in the most exclusive shopping areas, from Milan-Via Montenapoleone, to Paris-Rue du Faubourg St. Honoré, New York-Madison Avenue, Beverly Hills-Rodeo Drive, Hong Kong-Canton Road, Shanghai-Nanjing Road, Dubai-Dubai Mall and Mall of the Emirates, Moscow-Gum.

© Paul and Shark

# Chanel & Karl Lagerfeld

French designer Coco Chanel defined the world of fashion in terms of sports and sportswear. Gabrielle Chanel was a visionary who advocated a svelte and sporty silhouette free from clutter. The simple and easy-to-wear clothes she designed were outfits in which fluidity was as much suited to sport as to travelling or everyday life. From then on, the world of sport was forever entwined with that of Chanel. Gabrielle Chanel used to say 'I invented the sports' dress for myself; not because other women played sports, but because I did. I didn't go out because I needed to design dresses, I designed dresses precisely because I went out, because I have lived the life of the century, and was the first to do so.'

She was an accomplished horseback rider, golfer and skier as well as a fishing, sailing and hunting enthusiast. She had an intuition for the sporting influence on fashion before anyone else. Gabrielle Chanel discovered sports with Etienne Balsan, a horse enthusiast who opened the doors for her to the racecourse and stud farms, and introduced her to riding in 1906. Two years later, she met Boy Capel, an English businessman who would become the great love of her life. He was a fervent horseman and keen polo player himself. The designer would further cultivate her love of horses with the Duke of Westminster. It made perfect sense that she should design riding trousers adapted to her own needs. And jersey was her discovery. In 1913, Gabrielle Chanel opened a boutique in Deauville, where she had noticed the jersey tops worn by the fishermen. The following year, this fabric, which allows greater freedom of movement, appeared in her collections. The success of Gabrielle Chanel's sports clothes was such that in 1921 a sports atelier was created within the House. Coats, tennis dresses with a boat neck, soft suits, and sweaters for golf and the beach were all inspired by the personal wardrobe of Gabrielle Chanel. During their time together from 1920-1930, Gabrielle Chanel and the Duke of Westminster alternated

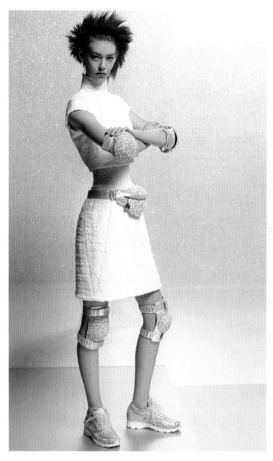

© Chanel

between yachting, hunting, fishing and rounds of golf. When she spent her winters in Saint-Moritz at the beginning of the 1930s, Gabrielle Chanel would ski in whipcord trousers and polo neck sweaters with ribbed cuffs and waist. Then for summer and yachting, Mademoiselle Chanel proposed swimming costumes, bathing dresses, as well as fluid beachwear.

Sports play an equally important role in the work of Lagerfeld. By translating the vision of a wardrobe that combines the masculine and feminine, and both casual and sophisticated lines, Karl Lagerfeld turned his attention to horse riding, golf, tennis, fishing, skiing, surfing, badminton, fencing, cycling, running, boxing and even the gym.

In his A/W 84/85 Ready-to-Wear collection, Karl Lagerfeld reinvented fisherman's waterproofs with an ultra-feminine version: a yellow canvas trouser and cape suit, and a quilted and pearl bag. For the Spring-Summer 1997 Ready-to-Wear collection floral jodhpurs and military jackets were reminders of Gabrielle Chanel's passion for horses. For Spring-Summer 2006, we were introduced to a little cropped jacket with quilted sleeves worn with a 'double C' stamped riding hat. For the Fall-Winter 1994/95 Ready-to-Wear collection, Karl Lagerfeld drew his first silhouettes dedicated to the mountains: over-sized fur collars, parkas with large collars and braided jackets accessorised with multi-coloured ski-googles set the tone and gave winter sports outfits an elegant allure. We see a boxer's silhouette in head-to-toe red leather for Fall-Winter 1992/93, and a more sober version in shorts and gilet braided in black and grey for Spring-Summer 2006. Surfing made an appearance in the Spring-Summer 1991 collection when Karl Lagerfeld sent his first surfboard down the runway with a wetsuit, humorously mixing cycling shorts with a sparkling jacket. Lagerfeld dedicated his Spring-Summer 2012 campaign to sport and called it 'Chanel Athletics': the black and white visuals in a purified décor presented the collection with sports equipment including the pommel horse, parallel bars, trapeze, rings, etc. For Spring-Summer 2014 Haute Couture he imagined a corseted silhouette finished with sneakers, uniting the ultimate symbol of femininity with that of androgynous sportswear.

Chanel's sportswear vision, Haute Couture, and prêt-à-porter relate to each other through Karl Lagerfeld's creative prism which turned sportswear into an essential part of the female wardrobe. Lagerfeld says: 'Today, sport is a source of inspiration for fashion, as it is for the streets. What can fashion give sport? Better made and better cut clothes. You have to create the sorts of clothes that women need. Fashion isn't just about suits, dresses and evening gowns. Everyone goes skiing and has to wear appropriate clothing. These days sports clothes must be easy to wear and in fashion. They are worn just as much in town with a pair of jeans, as in the countryside, in the cold and rain. It's the sport attitude.'

# AMERICAN FOOTBALL

**Who does not know the sport with the oval-shaped football?** American football is the most popular sport in the United States. Millions play the game in the States and around the world. The Super Bowl ranks among the most-watched club sporting events in the world and the sport is the most profitable in North America. The National Football League, the most popular American football league, has the highest average attendance of any sports league in the world. American football, referred to as football in the United States and Canada, is also known as gridiron. It is a sport played by two teams of eleven players. The sport is played on a rectangular field with goalposts at each end. The game is between the offence the team with control of the ball and trying to advance down the field by running and passing the ball, and the *defence* or the team aiming to stop their advance and take control of the ball for themselves. The offence must advance at least ten yards in four downs, or else they turn over the football to the opposing team; if they succeed, they are given a new set of four downs. The players score by advancing the ball into the opposing team's end zone for a touchdown. The winning team has the most points at the end of a game.

The attraction of the game lies in the fact that any person (fat, thin, large or small) can have a role in the game and can make the difference in the game. American Football is a true team-sport because 11 players interact and pass on the ball to each other. Every player is the link in a chain of 11 players who work together to score a touchdown. American Football allows anyone to play and embodies a true American team spirit which attracts many boys and girls to this sport.

© Under Armour

## Under Armour is the youngest and maybe the strongest newcomer in sportswear

The origin of American Football lies in the history of sports in college. The first game of American football was played on November 6, 1869, between two college teams, Rutgers and Princeton, under rules based on the association football rules of the time. In the late 1900s teams playing American football switched to the Rugby Union code, which allowed carrying the ball. A set of rule changes was drawn up from 1880 onwards by Walter Camp, who established the snap, eleven-player teams, and the concept of the down.

**UNDER ARMOUR**

In 1996, Kevin Plank, a 23-year old former University of Maryland special teams captain, turned an idea born on the football field into a new industry that changed the way athletes dress forever. Back in his playing days, Plank hated having to change his sweat-soaked cotton T-shirts over and over again. Knowing that there simply had to be an alternative, he set out to create a solution. Plank named his new company Under Armour, and after extensive research on the athletic benefits of synthetic fabrics, he designed the first Under Armour HeatGear T-shirt, which he named the number 0037. Engineered with moisture-wicking performance fibres, the shirt helped keep athletes cool, dry, and light in the most brutally hot conditions.

Working from his grandmother's basement in Washington DC's Georgetown neighbourhood, he travelled up and down the East Coast selling his revolutionary new product out of the boot of his car. By the end of 1996, Plank made his first team sale, and Under Armour generated $17,000 in sales.

In 1997, Under Armour introduced the now-famous ColdGear fabric, which keeps athletes warm, dry, and light in cold conditions, and then the AllSeasonGear line, which keeps athletes comfortable between the extremes.

By the end of 1998, Under Armour had outgrown grandma's basement and moved to an all-new headquarters and warehouse in Baltimore. In 1999, Under Armour played a supporting role in one of the year's most talked about movies, *Any Given Sunday,* starring Al Pacino and Jamie Foxx. In the film, the football team wears Under Armour apparel and accessories in key scenes.

Over the next two years, the brand formed relationships with key retail partners and professional sports leagues such as Major League Baseball, the National Hockey League, and the Baltimore Marathon. In 2002, to support its continued growth, the brand moved its global headquarters to an old soap factory in the Tide Point section of south Baltimore.

Under Armour had its first ever TV campaign using Maryland football standout Eric 'Big E' Ogbogu, and a group of young athletes forming the voice of a generation that officially made the brand a household name. Under Armour launched a women's line, UA Women, in 2003. Under Armour Golf was introduced in 2005. Plank signed his first all-school deal with the University of Maryland.

On November 18, 2005, Under Armour went public and became the first US-based initial public offering in five years to double on its first day of trading. Over the years, Under Armour has made significant strides in establishing a strong presence outside of the US. Through on-field partnerships with elite professional teams and players, the brand gained attention all over the world. In 2011, Under Armour opened its first-ever brand store in

China and became the official technical partner of Tottenham Hotspur of the Barclays Premier League. Under Armour has celebrated partnerships with top athletes Michael Phelps, Ray Lewis and Tom Brady.

The brand's mission is to make all athletes better through passion, design, and the relentless pursuit of innovation. UA has a mission to countless game-changing products that gives athletes an advantage. Founder Kevin Plank evolved from a man with an idea to help football players improve, into a global leader in performance footwear, apparel and accessories. Plank is still determined to make all athletes perform better and does this through his dedication to build tomorrow's next great innovations. Under Armour also expanded all over the world and opened its European headquarters in the Old Olympia Stadium.

Today, Under Armour is a leading developer, marketer, and distributor of branded performance apparel, footwear, equipment, and connected fitness platforms. The brand offers state-of-the-art products designed to help athletes perform better, including innovative footwear, moisture-wicking and temperature-regulating apparel for men, women, and youth, as well as digital fitness mobile applications. While the technology behind Under Armour's diverse product assortment has grown significantly, the performance apparel platform that started it all is based on a simple concept: wear HeatGear® when it's hot, ColdGear® when it's cold, and AllSeasonGear® between the extremes.

In June 2006, Under Armour entered the footwear business with the launch of a football cleat line, and later introduced baseball, softball cleats and basketball shoes in 2011. In 2012, the Brand launched a new footwear technology, UA Spine, offering the fusion of flexibility and ultimate lightweight structure underfoot. In 2014, Under Armour's SpeedForm Apollo running shoe, the first footwear to be developed in an apparel factory, was named as "Best Debut" by *Runner's World* Magazine. Building on the success of the SpeedForm footwear platform, the brand released the UA SpeedForm Gemini in 2015. The SpeedForm Gemini brings precision fit and feel to a shoe made for long distance running. It features a seamless heel cup and lightweight, breathable upper, which minimises distractions and allows for a more locked in, personalised fit.

Under Armour also offers sports equipment, including athletic performance gloves, bags, headwear, socks, eyewear, and performance mouth guards.

# Tommy Hilfiger

American designer Tommy Hilfiger looks back at a successful career spanning more than thirty years. Celebrating this milestone in 2016, Hilfiger reveals to me how he enrolled in fashion.

'I grew up in Elmira, a small town in upstate New York. When I was a teenager I fell in love with rock and roll and wanted to be a rock star, except I couldn't play an instrument. I decided to try and look the part instead, but the styles I wanted weren't available in Elmira, so it became my new dream to develop very cool, rock and roll-inspired clothing. When I was 18, I opened my first store, People's Place, where we sold bell bottoms and fashion that hadn't been seen in our small town before. It laid the foundation for my career and confirmed that designing was my true passion. Soon after that, I moved to New York City and in 1985 I founded the Tommy Hilfiger brand.'

Mr. Hilfiger has had an interest in sports from the very beginning. He explains how he chose American football as his favourite sport and image creator. 'I've always been inspired by sport – when I was a kid I dreamed of becoming a professional football player, but I was too small. However, I remained fascinated by sports uniforms, and this inspiration is often part of my collections. I love the details like badges, sporty fabrics, contrast stitching and bold lettering.'

Hilfiger reveals how his career in fashion evolved into the direction of sportswear and casual. 'I founded my brand in 1985, and from the beginning my goal has always been to give a modern West Coast-inspired twist to classic East Coast style. As we've grown into a global brand, the "classic American cool" look and feel has remained at the heart of our signature style.'

How does he define sportswear? 'Our sportswear collections are a fusion of casual, all-American classics that are easy, effortless, everyday staples. The look is relaxed and youthful but authentic, cool and sophisticated at the same time.'

© Tommy Hilfiger

Building up a brand such as Tommy Hilfiger has taken years of planning. 'We just celebrated the thirtieth anniversary of our brand, and it's been an incredible journey. Our success has come from defining a clear brand DNA and staying true to this heritage over the years. We're driven to celebrate individuality and break conventions while never losing our inclusive, optimistic spirit. We have also embraced digital innovation in all areas of our business, and use technology as a tool to democratise fashion and share it with people all over the world.'

# Style is about dressing with confidence, whether you are in the office or on the soccer pitch

What are his best memories of the Hilfiger brand over the years? 'Many of my favourite memories are tied to our amazing partnerships with celebrities, musicians and influencers, from sponsoring the Rolling Stones "No Security" tour in 1999, working with Beyoncé on my True Star perfume, to recently announcing Gigi Hadid as our new women's ambassador.'

Hilfiger stresses the importance of sport to his brand: 'The links between sport and fashion are well established, and I don't want to split the two worlds. I really like the idea that an item of clothing can be worn in the city and on a sports field, and that the lining of a preppy jacket can be made from a really technical type of fabric. Adding a touch of sport to collections gives "luxe" a new lease of life.'

For Mr. Hilfiger the ultimate sport is tennis: 'My favourite sport is tennis. Rafael Nadal is our global brand ambassador for our men's tailored, underwear and fragrance collections, and I have huge respect for him as one of the greatest athletes of his generation.'

How important is style for sportswear? 'Style is about dressing with confidence, whether you're at the office, on the soccer pitch, or heading to a red carpet event.'

**www.lannoo.com**

Register on our website to receive regular newsletters with
information on new books and interesting, exclusive offers.

**Text:** Leen Demeester
**Lay-out:** Studio Lannoo
**Cover image:** © Under Armour
**Back cover:** © Puma (left), © Hacket (middle), © Bogner (right)

If you have comments or questions, please contact our
editing department at redactielifestyle@lannoo.com

© Lannoo Publishers nv, Tielt, Belgium, 2016
D/2016/45/238 – NUR452
ISBN 978 94 014 3673 1